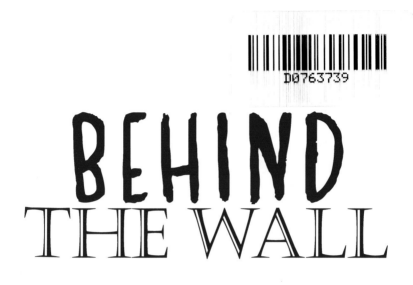

BEHIND THE WALL

by

Connie Steinman

DORRANCE
PUBLISHING CO
EST. 1920
PITTSBURGH, PENNSYLVANIA 15238

Editor: Scott Steinman
Cover Designer: Rebeca @Rebecacovers

Dorrance Publishing Co
585 Alpha Drive
Pittsburgh, PA 15238
Visit our website at *www.dorrancebookstore.com*

ISBN: 978-1-6853-7442-6
eISBN: 978-1-6853-7586-7

REVIEWS
Behind the Wall

I read your book cover to cover yesterday and found it both saddening and uplifting. As a leader in my organization championing Diversity, Equity, and Inclusion efforts, I have long known the unfairness in how our world treats, and in fact creates, marginalized urban youth. I applaud the courage it took to put on paper your struggles with what is arguably the most crucial, and yet least valued, profession—as well as your getting into the trenches every day to make a difference. Your honesty gives witness to what is important in life, the timeless impact of well-considered literature, and how the passion I saw in you at FIT still tills fertile, if a bit rocky, soil. You personify the philosophy so important to Mandela and Tutu— "Ubuntu." You may know the term, but if not, it is a Nguni Bantu (Zulu) word that has been translated as "I am because we are" or "the belief in a universal bond of sharing that connects all humanity." It recognizes that none of us can truly fulfill our role as human beings without serving those around us. Publishing a book like you have extends "those around us" to anyone who reads the book. Thank you!
—Steve Small, Architecture/Professor

Behind the Wall by Connie Steinman follows a diversely populated suburban city high school with underprivileged students who learn life skills, coping skills, and self-reliance through the lessons of Emerson, taught by a teacher who encourages them to look within to persevere and to beat the odds. Connie connects and inspires James and his friends who are credit deficient to graduate! This is a book about teaching, learning, and self-reliance. It contains a lesson for all of us.

"The details which you describe your students is amazing.
I get a perfect picture" —Kevin Wagoner

"Behind the Wall by Connie Steinman touches your heart and
tells the life challenges of poverty with today's youth"
—Amazon Customer

Kudos to Connie for writing this book and sharing what some school systems are dealing with. And for her perseverance with the students in helping them to believe in themselves and make it to graduation. Teachers are unsung heroes, and especially ones working in schools that don't give much support. And with her hearing problem, I would have thought most people would have quit long ago. Thank you Connie, for not giving up on today's kids and for sharing your experience!
—Mauricio Gonzalez

I loved the Emerson readings that Connie gave her students to help her connect with each and everyone one of them!
And that they appreciated her for her teachings!!
—Linda Glossner

ACKNOWLEDGMENTS

I want to thank the ASL III class, 3rd period, 2018-2019, for inspiring
and encouraging me! Thank you, Mariam Abdel-Gwad, Daylisha Asberry,
Hero Do, Sofia Johnson, Regina McDaniel, Kayla Saeteurn,
Tui Saukuru, Lillian Xiong, and Alyssia Ybarra.
I also want to thank the ASL II/III class of 2012 and the
ASL II class of 2014, who gave me many ideas from which to write.

Thank you, Angel Thacker, my writing and spiritual coach,
for guiding me and navigating the challenges in organizing my story.

Thank you, Elise Devereux and Lynne Ruvalcaba, for supporting me
during incredibly challenging teaching assignments and classes!

Thank you, Joel Foote, Lisa Hall, Christa Hewett, Mike Lauchli,
Peter Matthiesen, Brendan Murphy, Scott Steinman,
and Shannon Fouchard for listening and your support!

Thank you, Annette Manolis for believing in me!
Thank you to my brother, Scott Steinman and Dorothy Ochotny.
Their input proved to be instrumental to my final draft!

Thank you for your donations toward publishing!

Beth Bergen, Julie Bosch, Michael Crooks, Jonathan Kern, David Keyzer,
Dede Lindgren, Bonnie Neff, Marco Palilla, Scott and Tracy Rauschkolb,
Johnny Salatlam, Dee Strayner, John Stroud, and Kate Tharp.

TABLE OF CONTENTS

FOREWORD
Angel Thacker, Joyous Life Coach

I met Connie Steinman at a holistic conference some years back, where she came to me for coaching. At the time, I wasn't aware that she was a school teacher. She had a warm spirit, a desire to learn, and a deep need to be part of something special. She somehow felt she wasn't given enough or doing enough in life. She just didn't know what or where she could make this difference. As I came to know her, she revealed that she was one of the unsung heroes of our modern times. An individual committed to serving the community as a high school teacher. I remember my first thought, for she wasn't like most of the people you know, for Connie lived most of her life with a hearing impairment. She wore a hearing aid and had a slight speech impediment due to the level of her hearing loss. This had to be challenging to navigate through in a room filled with high school students. I imagined she had a difficult job and perhaps even hated her job. That was just me seeing her life through my personal filters.

You see, I remember high school. I remember how hard it was for me. As a timid, nerdy young girl, I was not exactly treated with kindness and warmth. I was bullied and harassed mercilessly and often wanted to drop out of school so that I didn't have to deal with the bullies. For children can be unkind at this age. It affected me well into my adult life for some time. One could say I didn't really begin pulling out of my shell until well into my thirties, doing the work to let go of and heal from the terrors of high school. I do remember one light that shined in my experience, something that helped me stay the course, and that was my high school physics teacher, Mr. Weary. He always helped me be proud of who I was, the brain in my head, and the ambitions of flying to the moon. Though my life's path didn't travel the road to NASA, I do have a strong sense of pride in who I am. Much of which is because of the one teacher who saw my need for support and kindness and stepped in.

Working with Connie caused me to think about my high school experience and how important my physics teacher was to me. As she spoke about her dream to write a book, I was intrigued at the thought of seeing the classroom experience through the eyes of a teacher. I jumped at the opportunity to help her focus and gave her some encouragement and a shoulder – something every writer can use. What I was expecting was another book about how a teacher changed the lives of a group (or one) of rowdy kids by helping them see the importance of education, and how they all skipped happily down the road to success at the end. That was not her story. For her, this was not a conversation about all the good she did; this was a celebration of the students she loved and the struggles of teaching in today's political and economic environment through an educator's eyes.

She has an interesting way to reach her students, using the writings of the great poet Ralph Waldo Emmerson. An author whose work kept her focused on not giving up and, through her focus, gave a sense of purpose and responsibility to her small group of students. The stories she shares are both inspirational and poignant. She writes with courage and no filter. You see what our teachers face in their struggle to create a positive and powerful experience for her class, all while wrestling with no books, disengaged parents, criminal elements, and more. How the administration can create blocks when there should be cooperation, and how politics and history can affect the destiny of a generation of students who had no skin in the game but have to live with the struggle. This book is real talk.

Connie has been through some of her tragedies that have given her cause to refocus her life. Like so many of us, she is ready to make a difference and roar to the wind. I am proud and profoundly impressed with Connie's revelation of how hard it is, not just for the teachers, but for the students. She speaks of her students as if they were her children. The only regrets she shares are those that she sees as a failure. Where she feels that she could have done more, the thing is, she walked into our high school teaching system and made that difference she was looking so hard for. You did it, Connie, and you did it well.

INTRODUCTION

Why did I write this book? It began with a traumatic health event that left me unconscious on life support. After the doctors brought me out of the coma, I found a new appreciation for life and decided to share my story. This book consolidates twenty years of moments woven into a patchwork story depicting my tenure as a teacher in an inner-city high school in which I guide a classroom of behaviorally challenged misfits to graduation. With every child facing challenges including family health crisis, widespread poverty, gang affiliation, and personal loss, it feels as though every child is a problem child. I need to approach them with more than lesson plans. How do I get them to graduation?

After my hospital stay, I found myself housebound and between several therapists. I had time to go through my storage closet. While digging through some boxes, I unearthed a history of memories in my journal, old behavioral referral forms, printouts of emails, memos, letters to and from parents. Teaching a diverse population who vary economically, ethnically, academically, and culturally has been an adventure. At times, entertaining, frustrating, elating, and even heartbreaking.

Join me as I walk down memory lane introducing a host of vibrant characters and accompany us on our journey to graduation. I will share the pitfalls of public education, paint a picture of the hostile environment we are all forced to survive, and divulge salacious secrets of the staff. Centered on my efforts with a particularly difficult group of students, through a very hard year, we examine Ralph Waldo Emerson's "Self-Reliance" essay and follow this English class through their trials and triumphs of their high school experience. Several of these students barely made it out of high school with a diploma and one did not make it out alive. In this story, I grow as a teacher who reconnects with my students after losing faith in the system. I myself take accountability for feeling discouraged until a colleague helps me renew my spirit of teaching. My revived enthusiasm for teaching encourages my students to think outside the box and become responsible for their actions and choices. My students examine their reality and become great thinkers of their generation.

Publishing my first book has been a tremendous achievement. I was born Deaf with an 85% decibel hearing loss and had been prescribed medication for OCD. I was overweight and recently separated. Then, as previously mentioned, in August 2018, I entered a floatation tank and suddenly slipped into a coma for five days. The doctors suspected that a heart attack caused the coma. When the staff found me floating limp, I was rushed to the hospital where I stayed in intensive care for ten days. I suffered from a traumatic brain injury, had cardiac complications, and was not responsive to stimuli. The doctors explained to my friends and family that there was a high probability that I wasn't going to make it and to be prepared. The only thing that I can remember from my time unconscious was seeing the color purple and hearing voices praying for me. I woke up five days later! I had medical leave for two months from my teaching position and in-home health care with several therapists: speech, mobility, and physical. All visited me individually once a week for six weeks. I had to learn to move around again. Friends had to drive me to appointments and errands for eight weeks. On top of all my other struggles my seventeen-year-old cat passed away. I was very depressed and at a low point in my life.

But as I healed body and mind, I began to feel that I was brought back for living my purpose in life. During my recovery, I made a lot of positive changes. My mental health improved and I lost sixty pounds. I purchased top of the line digital hearing aids for myself. My hearing went from less than 50% all of my life to hearing 98%. I was truly reborn. I count my blessings that I not only survived and got my mobility back. When I returned to work in October 2018, I knew that I had to finish this book. This incident woke me up and inspired me to act!

CHAPTER 1
James: Morning Conversations with Mom

Lost in her thoughts, Mariam Ward watched a typical dispute unfold outside her kitchen window while contemplating her latest dilemma with her son. Here in the Ghetto, abandoned cars line the street of worn-out houses with sheets used for drapes. Siblings share bedrooms and bathrooms with extended family members while contending with overcrowded living conditions. On hot summer nights, folks sit on the front porch smoking and playing cards. Gang bangers perch on the curb around the clock accosting pedestrians and passing traffic. Drug sales are the primary income for many in this neighborhood. Antiquated row homes hide behind rusty iron gates that no longer provide protection. Burned-out street lamps, liquor stores, broken bottles, and empty baggies dominate the landscape. Drive-bys occur daily. There is a violent turf war going on here. School is the safest place and only chance of escape for James and his friends.

Mariam Ward is tall, slender, beautiful, African American with big sparkling brown eyes. She could have been a model! She worked for the local electric company for fifteen years before her department downsized and cut her position. Now, at thirty-seven, she works in the computer department at Walmart. Dressed in her uniform, Mariam grips her mug in both hands and sips her coffee as a new stress-line forms on her brow. Staring out the window, Miriam reflects on the past with regret.

The fat Black lady next door is standing with her hands on her hips next to an old rusty Ford. The lady is shouting at her husband, who is backing the car off the front lawn. Mariam watched closely.

Interrupting her thoughts, her son James appears for breakfast. Despite his recent behavior, she couldn't help but notice his good looks. He is tall, thin, and dark brown, just like her. He brandishes a gold grill on his front teeth. He takes pride in his appearance and dresses in crisp denim and a white T-shirt. He is never without his oversized yellow headphones around his neck. Mariam stiffens and thinks, "The Lord makes him handsome so I don't kill him, doesn't he?"

"Morning, Mom." James, sits quickly, narrowly avoiding direct eye contact with his mother and places his headphones over his ears, not waiting for her reply like he doesn't have a clue, yet he is all too aware of the impending conflict.

Miriam stands motionless and returns his greeting with silence before turning from the window and slamming the empty coffee cup on the table. James jumps up from the sound. He looks at her and laughs nervously.

"What's up, Mom?" chewing his toast slowly and looking uneasy.

Miriam eyes him contemptuously. She seizes his headphones and tosses them on the table in front of him. James leans back in his chair, flushed.

"I am getting tired of your teachers and counselors calling me. You are supposed to be getting a decent education and making something of yourself."

"Yeah…I know Mom," he said, rolling his eyes.

"No, you don't!" his mother snapped, "I'm sick and tired of busting my ass so you can go fuck around at school…I don't need no more stress in my life, you feel me boy! And you bullying students… fucking around… having the school calling me…. stresses me the fuck out!" Miriam pulls out a crumpled letter and holds it up in front of James' face. "Explain this shit to me!"

"Mom I can…," he began. Knowing the paper before him would be a recounting of his latest shenanigans.

"Do not! Do not say one word. I am killing myself just trying to put food on our table and keep the bills paid! I want to see you succeed not waste it all away. When your father left…"

"Well, it is not my fault!" James interrupted.

"Nothing is your fault! I wish I finished my degree before I married your father and had a steady career. I thought I had it all figured out. You can't depend on shit. Can't even depend on you to act right in school."

James stared coldly at her. Mariam continued, "I'm gonna have to come down and watch your ass. You have to be responsible for your own actions. Things are gonna change TODAY!"

"Yeah, well I didn't do nothing! I hate that place!" James grabbed his backpack off the hook. Shoving the last of his toast in his mouth, James quickly left the house without looking back.

Furious, she slams her coffee cup into the sink, shattering it into a thousand pieces. Squeezing her head between her hands and pulling her hair, she prayed, "God please, I don't know what to do no more!" She wept heavily and threw her hands down, returning to the sink to pick up the shards. She felt like a failure. Mariam concluded her thought, "I hate this place as much as James hates school. I want to do right, but I'm out of options. Now I have to call his fucking counselor again! Take time off work that I can't afford to miss. James is on the wrong path. But how can he find the right one in this hell hole. Oh Jesus, please help me." She stood with her eyes closed, tears slowly trickling down her cheeks, silently waiting for a sign. Praying for a miracle.

CHAPTER 2
BD—A Senior in 9th Grade

BD Garcia is good-looking and muscular with a flawless black mohawk that's shiny, thick, and wavy. The girls love to run their fingers through his hair when he passes them in the hallway. He has a broad face with a million-dollar smile. BD has a movie star quality about him, like Newman or Brando, except BD is Mexican. He is a real punk rocker with black Doc Martens boots and multicolored laces. He clads cut-off jeans at the knees with long underwear beneath them and a denim jacket with torn off sleeves at the shoulders layered over an army green camouflaged t-shirt. He religiously wears his gold cross and chain, a gift from his mother. Zelda, a devout Christian, had BD later on in life than most mothers do. She is emaciated and her hair is prematurely turning grey and thinning. Zelda has stage 4 cancer that was diagnosed when she went to the doctor for a lump in her breast. BD missed a lot of school to care for her. He wants to spend as much time with her as he could.

BD is the youngest of his brothers who are now adults. His father was absent most of his life. BD's story is common amongst his peers with one exception. He scored top of his class, not only on the SAT, but also the college, military, and vocational tests. BD could have perused any academic, trade, or career opportunity and earned a free scholarship. He had potential. A lot of it! BD should have been a senior, but skipping classes and incomplete classwork had left him with a severe credit-deficiency that will hold him back another year if his disposition was left unaddressed. This is sad because he is smart, really smart for an eighteen- year- old in ninth grade. However, he lacks basic self-esteem and he has a sadness about him that is more than his mother's diagnosis.

BD and his mother live in a small two-bedroom, one bath apartment. Their apartment has minimal furniture and personal effects. They have a small altar in the living room and an obsolete television on top of a wooden crate in front of the couch. They depend on welfare. Their kitchen has a four-foot galley with a counter against the wall including a small round kitchen table for two opposite the counter.

The phone rang interrupting the silence. "Hello, Ms. Garcia. This is BD's English teacher, Ms. Steinman. I am calling to let you know about BD's performance."

"Oh, hi, Ms. Steinman. How is he doing now?"

"He is not doing well. He is failing my class, and I hate to tell you, he is also failing three others."

Through a muffled receiver, I heard Zelda's yelling at BD, "Your teacher is on the phone! How many times must I warn you to keep up on schoolwork; that's your priority!"

Zelda resumed, "I'm sorry he's been so busy taking care of my needs. My insurance doesn't cover an in-home nurse."

I reminded her, "BD got more smarts than most here but he needs to meet the credit requirements to graduate or he'll be forced to repeat again."

Zelda sobbed quietly. BD was blindsided by the call but not the news.

"I can't do it for you. I can't do it for you," she said.

I asked, "Zelda, do you think BD has depression or something? This is a lot for a student his age to shoulder. He clowns around at school, but I know there is more beneath the surface. I can put him in touch with counseling services."

Zelda admitted, "I don't know. Sometimes, I worry that he uses my illness as an excuse for not doing his schoolwork and smoking blunts with his boys. Maybe you are right though. Is there anything we can do about his grades?"

"BD could still give me assignments for full credit. I will contact his other teachers and ask for their input and try to set up a meeting," I offered.

"Wonderful, Ms. Steinman! I know we will work well together to help get BD where he needs to be, thank you for your commitment, talk soon."

Exhausted from the stir caused by the phone call, Zelda laid down on the couch and stared at the ceiling. Sweat beads formed on her forehead.

"BD, come close, I need to speak to you," she whispered faintly.

BD leaned close to her, "Yeah, Mama?"

"BD, don't worry, everything 'Mi Irie. Have faith. God has a plan for you even if you don't understand. Listen to your teacher. She is doing everything she can to help. You could be the first Garcia to graduate. Nothing would make me prouder of you, my son."

"Mama… this shit ain't fair! You are all I got. Faith? Faith in what? God takes whatever…" BD's voice began to quiver.

"Listen to me. I think your soul is in jeopardy. You must believe there is a greater plan at work and you have an important role in it. My cancer is aggressive and my prognosis, grim. I'm not going to bullshit you. This will be my last birthday spent with you. Last of everything. You are stronger than you give yourself credit for and smarter. But you will never be self-reliant without building a strong foundation and that needs to begin today. You are already working against the clock. So, what are you waiting for?"

"I can't, Mama!" BD rested his head on his mother's arm to hide his shame. His mom was right. It was now or never.

"Just start with catching up in school Son, please for me."

"I'll do my best."

BD headed off to meet James on the path to school. Both boys greeted each other casually; unaware of the others similar struggles.

"Yo, BD! What's up, Bro? Got that bleezy for the breazy?"

"Of course, James. Let's get behind that dumpster in the parking lot at Bel Air."

"Cool BD, very cool, I really need to chill!"

Behind the dumpster, BD lit up and each took a couple of tokes. James inhaled deeply and slowly released. "Man. I fuckin' hate that place. I already feel under the microscope from the teachers… and this guy, Amar, keeps looking at me in English like he likes me or something."

BD took the blunt. He exhaled several smoke rings slowly as he glanced at James. "Yeah, I know what you mean, he kind of looks at the teacher and everyone like that. It ain't about you."

"Well, he makes me feel uneasy, and I want to change seats."

"No reason to escalate things, James; Amar doesn't mean anything, he is in Special Ed."

"Yeah, and he is weird, always waving his hands and murmuring."

"Come on, James," BD motioned to leave, "he can't help it. He doesn't have it easy. He ain't cool like us! Let's keep it moving. We need to take on another day in that hell hole."

"You said it. So, how is your mom?"

"Man, it's rough! She is a fighter, though. I wish she wouldn't worry about me so much, though!"

"Well, at least she has you to take care of her. Too bad, that school will not put you in independent studies or home school... or something... this fucking place defies common sense," replied James.

The boys resumed their walk to school. Eve joined them when they arrived outside the PE gates.

"Did you save a hit for me?" she asked, sniffing the air.

"For sure!" BD pulled out the roach and lit it for her.

"That's what's up." Eve coughed and exhaled a thick cloud.

They joked and laughed as they entered the gates at school and James rapped to his friends. BD was glassy eyed and Eve strutted in a way which called attention to herself. The campus monitors Kiki and Cash honed in on their arrival and approached them.

"Hey, have you kids have been smoking?" Kiki leaned in to get a whiff, "Your clothes smell like weed."

"You reek like skunks," accused Cash.

James kept humming to his rap music unfazed. He raised his hands and shouted in sync with the rhythm, "Why do you keep fucking with me?" The others giggled.

Cash commanded, "Stop and empty your pockets, now."

They fished through their pockets. Eve had a few singles, James had nothing, and BD pulled out the lighter.

BD laughed, "We finished already! Too late."

Kiki finished patting them down and motioned to Cash that they were clean. Frustrated, Cash grumbled, "Give me that lighter and get to class."

As the kids brushed by them, Kiki shook her head and warned Cash that they couldn't do anything without evidence. It was difficult to intervene with students in a meaningful way and is the source of frustration to all the staff. Kiki and Cash preferred taking a lenient approach. It was easier to act like their buddy to gain compliance.

CHAPTER 3
Robin' the Hood

BD and James became close friends when they entered high school as freshmen. BD also met Manny, Eve, Jezebel, and Delilah that year. BD was respectful and liked by many of his teachers and lacked the long referral reports that his friends had racked up. BD smoked recreationally which on occasion had gotten him into some precarious situations!

I remember when these students had me for freshman English during fifth period after lunch, and they had cut class. This mischievous group left campus with plans to burglarize a house that was close to the school.

The tardy bell rang. I scanned the classroom noticing several of the students were out. I took roll call. Six absent students. "Has anybody seen James, BD, or Manny today?" The class shook their heads and looked at each other. "Has anyone seen Eve, Jez, or Del?" No confirmation. "Hmm."

I wondered where they are? This is no coincidence. Something is afoot.

Meanwhile, several blocks away, Manny hoisted Eve up to access an unlocked window.

BD scanned the alley and looked back at his friends as Eve's sneakers disappeared into the opening, "Are you sure about this? Guys?"

James glanced back. "Sure man, it's gonna be easy. Come on BD. We need you."

Eve opened the back door and signaled them to enter.

"Cool!" exclaimed Jez as they slipped inside and quietly closed the screen door behind them. BD had second thoughts as he watched his friends enter the house. Eve, Manny, and James rummaged through dresser drawers and closets tossing their contents onto the floor.

"Bingo!" yelled Jez. "Look what we got here."

In her hand, she held a sandwich bag stuffed with large green buds and a fist full of cash.

"Yo. Check this out." James drew attention to a glass bong on the coffee table. "Now we got something to smoke that shit out of."

Del stood in front of the mirror admiring the earrings she swiped off the bathroom counter and spouted, "Check this shit out."

They regrouped in the kitchen. James unplugged a clock radio that sat atop of the fridge. "I could use one of these. Mine's broke."

At that moment, the front door unlocked. Jezebel's eyes widened. James raised his index finger to his lips. Jez looked at Manny. Without a word they darted towards the back door. Eve knocked over a lamp and stumbled and landed on her knees.

A gravely man's voice shouted out, "Who's there? I have a gun!" Del screamed. Jez jumped to her feet and caught up with the rest of them.

At that point, a gun shot rang out. It was impossible to tell if it came from inside or the street and it had less importance as they ran off. Several blocks away they stopped and caught their breath.

"That was close. You hear that gat?" asked Jez.

"Word. I shit myself." James fans his nose.

"Now what?" asks Eve.

"Let's drop some cheddar at Sev," suggested Manny.

They exited the alley, slapping each other on the back and turned onto MLK Boulevard going towards the 7-11. From behind, a police siren chirped twice.

All six of my students were suspended for three days including BD who never entered the home.

CHAPTER 4
Manny—Stoned Out!

Manny Wells is 5'8." He is a light-skinned Black with a muscular, slim build and a huge curly Afro-hairstyle the size of a large beach ball. Manny has two younger sisters and two older brothers. His mother works at a local Starbucks, one of his brothers works as a mechanic, and the other sells marijuana on the streets. One sister attends middle school, and the other is a sophomore in high school. His brothers bring home most of the money for his family to survive on. Unfortunately, his older brother, who sells pot, also gives Manny whatever he wants. Manny has been smoking heavily since junior high school, and he is glassy-eyed most of the time. The only two classes he passed in junior high was PE and art. Manny was suspended more times than any other student for a litany of infractions ranging from possession of marijuana or a knife in his backpack to fighting or encouraging others to follow his behavior. Maybe he should have gone to a rehab. He would have been a completely different person if he never smoked pot. He is one of James' close friends. Manny is also in love with Donna, an honors student in my English class. I am fairly certain that he is not her type. She aspires to earn a scholarship to Xavier College, a prestigious all-Black school.

I gave an assignment to Manny and James to draw something falling from the sky on the board. In an attempt to amuse James, he drew a hand with a middle finger in the sky. When I walked over, he crossed it out and started erasing it with his hand. I told him that I refused to accept that assignment and that he would have to do it again. He became agitated as James smirked at him.

Most of Manny's interaction with the girls has made them feel uncomfortable. For example, he has hugged too long and pressed his body against them and blocked their path with his legs. Although, it appeared as if they were playing around, I could see in their eyes that they were uneasy. I realized that these young girls did not standup for themselves. They have not learned to trust themselves, understand their value, or speak up for themselves. Overbearing parents raised daughters who looked to others for validation and self-approval.

On the other hand, sons who received no parental guidance engaged in unacceptable behavior as adults. Then these girls are dismissed as being the source of the problem instead of the instigator.

As a Deaf teenager, I lacked the self-confidence needed to fend off bullies. My high school friends shielded me. I sought out the opinion and validation of others well into adulthood. Our school needs a better support system that teaches students to make smarter decisions and think for themselves.

I witnessed these girls push Manny away and dodge his advances. I intervened and warned him to respect their personal space. He complied, but obviously the girls felt berated even more so when they failed to express it. I told Manny that he needed to pay attention to their body language. He argued, "You don't understand my relationship with them. They are not uncomfortable, you are!"

"Your intentions could be misconstrued as sexual harassment. You need to be mindful of how you treat others," I warned sternly.

"I will do what I want! You can't do jack about it!" Manny threatened.

"I am trying to show you how things can be misinterpreted." I reported his behavior and emailed his mother. His mother thanked me for the update and said she would talk to him. *This is a prime example of what happens when a mother works long hours, and there is no father figure in the house.*

Unfortunately, Manny's behavior was not an isolated one. Later that day, I attended an administrative behavioral meeting for another young Black male student. This meeting was between the student, his parents, all of his teachers, the disciplinary VP's, the nurse, the psychologist, and the healthy start coordinator. In the meeting, we addressed sexual harassment. The student had a well- documented track record for unsolicited vulgarity aimed at female students and staff. The latest incident involved him slapping a female teacher on her ass. He asked, "What are you going to do about it?"

When that teacher spoke at the meeting, she said, "You know, you think you are a cute boy now, but in a few years, at age eighteen, you will be seen as a young man. If you behave like this at work, you will be facing charges for sexual harassment, and you will have a criminal record. This act will make your future difficult. Believe me; I am worried for you!" She looked distraught at the student's mother. The staff who surrounded him found it difficult to make direct eye contact. The room was silent. Everyone felt uneasy.

Abruptly, the intervention was truncated by a commotion in the hall. Jill, Jean, and Shae were disoriented and stumbled outside of the meeting room.

As I stepped into the hall, James and Manny pointed at the three normally reserved girls who were gasping for air from their involuntary giggling outburst. Students and staff crowded around. The girls could not compose themselves.

I was confused. "What is going on here?"

James covered his mouth and mumbled to Manny, "They really enjoyed your magic brownies. They ate the entire box!" Manny dismissively motioned to James to cease talking. Suddenly, Jean's laughing halted, and she turned green. She projectile vomited all over Jill that sent Shae into another explosion of laughter as the crowd either gasped, wretched, or laughed.

"Okay, enough! Back to class now!" I instructed as the students began to disperse. The girls were escorted to the nurse, and Manny was taken to the principal for questioning. Shortly after, an ambulance arrived to rush the girls to the hospital. No one noticed. Sirens were commonplace.

Jean's uncle called Principal Smith inquiring why the school had not warned him about pot brownies when he enrolled Jean. Her uncle said that she denied knowing who gave it to her. Principal Smith assured him that she did. When the police officer finally searched Manny that day, he was in possession of a knife and a home-made pot pipe. Mr. Green called Manny's mother at work. He was suspended for five days. Expulsion would have

CHAPTER 5
Eve of Destruction

Eve Sanchez has long, frizzy hair, brown eyes, and dark brown skin. Eve is beautiful with a wide-tooth smile. She is what you might consider as thick, neither thin nor obese. She spent six months in juvenile hall the previous year for shoplifting $600 worth of jewelry from a department store in the downtown plaza. Her father served time in prison for grand theft auto. Eve is the oldest of six children and a dreadful role model for her younger siblings. Her father is from Mexico, and he had a son with his ex-girlfriend. Her father left that woman with his son, moved to California, and married her mother who is Black. Her older half-brother, who is a full-blooded Mexican, joined a Mexican gang. Her father wants no business in gang activity after serving time in prison. Her half-brother was kicked out of the house several years ago and lives with another gang member's family.

Eve has been pressured to join their gang. While walking to school, Eve has to be aware of her surroundings. She intentionally obscures her vulnerability by walking behind trees, garbage cans, or dodging between traffic if she suspects that she is being tailed. The female gang members want her loyalty. The gang offers Eve companionship, protection, a sense of belonging, and money. Eve has low self-esteem and doesn't know what she wants for herself; these feelings entice her desire to join. She believes she can find what she needs from outside of herself rather than from within. Her parents are adamantly opposed to gangs, and her father is strict. Eve sees how hard her parents work to keep their family intact. Her parents are responsible and well-educated. But Eve did not want to be the eldest one setting an example. She wants her freedom with no responsibility or accountability. Eve felt stuck in this situation with no way out!

Eve had me for an English class that went on a field trip to a Shakespeare play. I picked her up at home; otherwise, she wouldn't have been able to join us. I drove up to her street, and it was blocked in the middle by two cars. I waved my hand, and the cars backed up, allowing me to pass through. I pulled in front of her house and called her on my cell phone. She waited in the house, looking out her window. She scurried out of her home while her mother watched her get into my car without incident. We drove off. I did not feel secure until we were several minutes away.

Eve had changed a lot since she started high school. Once she started cavorting with James' and his friends she began smoking weed, skipping classes, and stealing. In a sense, she was obeying her parents' rule about not joining a gang! They didn't say she could not join a clique.

Eve became increasingly defiant in my class. During my lectures, she would talk over my instruction and make distracting noises. When I called on her, she would pretend to be helping a student next to her. During a PowerPoint lecture, when others were taking notes, Eve slipped out of class and hugged a student who was milling about in the hallway. When I tried to address her behavior, she refused to listen, faked a dramatic yawn, and popped her middle finger at the class and me! Over the four years I have taught Eve, she refused to put her cell phone away, marked her desk with gang symbols, snapped her pencils into pieces, and threw them at others. She has unplugged my computer keyboard and monitor. She has groomed a student's hair in the middle of the class, ignoring the lesson and my authority. When I questioned what she thought she was doing she answered back, "What is your problem?" oblivious to her disruptive behavior.

Once, she stood up and kicked a boy in the nuts, and I had to call the nurse! She shouted at him while he cupped his groin, "You're Hella weak! You ain't a man."

Her mother talked to Eve on the classroom phone; Eve hung up on her and left class to meet up with Manny. Eve has been caught arguing in the girls' bathroom exchanging insults and threats, fist fighting in the cafeteria, yelling into a class then running into another and addressing a teacher as her girlfriend. Eve knew better than anyone how much chaos she caused!

Eve joined the wrestling team for a semester and was part of a fundraiser in which she did not bring back the fundraiser money from the candy sales. Eve made a lot of excuses why she did not bring it back.

I realized how much her interest in gangs increased when I witnessed a campus fight after lunch. I knew as soon as I got out of my car that something was wrong. When I saw hundreds of Blue and Red gang members locked in a deadly staring contest where the loser is the first to blink. The entire staff watched as the tension mounted. Security monitored the situation from a distance and listened to law enforcement on their radio. Eve stood under a tree near my car. She wanted to be part of the excitement. A mass of students thundered past me headed toward the classrooms. Teachers scattered to avoid an impending collision. Hundreds of students scaled the back fence on River Street, landing on parked cars and denting their roofs. Hatred shining in their eyes. The Reds and the Blues are at war! Cop cars pulled in from every direction and handcuffed students. A boy was found beaten unconscious lying face down on River Street. His assailant was never identified.

"They found a gun on campus! Someone has a gun!" shouted a teacher.

"All the Mexicans have guns!" a student answered. Eve was still standing under a tree, unsure of herself as I headed back to my classroom.

Ironically, Eve is in the Police Academy. These classes are offered for students who aspire to study law enforcement in college. Maybe she thought they could protect her? The Police Academy has a substantial academic program with a free snack program, their own social events, mentors, field trips, and classes that interests her. Eve is bright, but she doesn't believe in herself, like most of my students. They don't understand how much they have to offer at that age.

CHAPTER 6
Jezebel's Hell

Jezebel is Black. She was adopted as an infant with her two older siblings who were ages two and four. Her biological mother was a crack head and each sibling had a different father. Her father left her mother before she was born. The state put Jezebel's mother in a rehabilitation clinic while the children were forced into foster care. Her mother had severe mental issues and could not stay clean so the state had to step in and permanently institutionalize her.

Delores is also Black and was in her mid-50s when she adopted Jezebel's family. Her husband died of cancer a few years before, and she had four children of her own. Her two oldest daughters were out on their own and her two younger sons were in junior high school. Delores operated a daycare from her home. Delores loves children and enjoyed having them around.

A few years after adopting Jezebel, Delores completely lost her vision. Her two younger sons were in high school and Jezebel was almost three. Managing her daycare from home was challenging and even more so because she could not see her kids now. Her life had become more demanding. Her younger sister, Belinda, came by to help. Belinda thought that her sister needed to make some changes. The home was chaotic and crowded and being blind became an obstacle.

As Jezebel grew up, she became aware that Delores couldn't see what she was up too. Jez's biological mother's drug usage during pregnancy affected Jezebel's chemistry and mental health since birth.

In elementary school, Jez started lying, cheating, and stealing. As she continued through grade school, it became evident that Jezzie suffered from a split personality. She was diagnosed as schizophrenic and prescribed medication. At home, she hid the children's toys, she lashed out physically, and she responded to voices in her head. Jezebel experienced dramatic mood swings. Delores could not see this and would dote on her. When Jezebel moved on to junior high, she began making faces and used gestures in disagreement with Delores. Delores never knew this.

By the time Jezebel entered high school, she was on a high dosage of medications for different mental issues. She also had a behavior IEP (Individual Educational Plan) with the resource department. Belinda observed Jez's manipulative behaviors on many occasions. She advised her sister to shut down the daycare, hire an in-home health aid to care for her, and apply for more state funding or welfare. But she never did.

When Jezebel was still in elementary school, her youngest step-brother received the largest life-time academic scholarship to attend the college of his choice and earn up to a PhD. During the summer season, her stepbrother worked at the corner barbershop. He was the kind of person who inspired others.

When he returned after his sophomore year of college to work, he was mistaken for a gang member. While he was cutting a man's hair, a car full of gangsters leaned out their window as they drove by and shot him through the glass storefront. Jezebel's stepbrother lay in a pool of his own blood. Later, the suspects were found, and they realized he wasn't the person they were after. Delores was never the same after that. She let her kids run wild.

James and Jez have been friends since middle school. She had a crush on him. James knew this, but he held firm they were only friends. He would lead her on, allowing her to do things for him, and then he would cast her aside until next time. Jezebel became skillful at manipulating Delores and her teachers.

Jezebel is unlike any student I have known. She has experienced great losses and dealt with them in some unusual ways. Her cousin was shot down in the neighborhood park. She came into class the day after the funeral. "Hey, Ms. Steinman, check this out!" Jezebel waves her cell phone wildly back and forth. She shows me a photo on her phone of a young Black man's head resting on a pillow. He is dressed in a suit asleep.

"Who is he?" I asked.

"My cousin. He's in a coma," Jezebel giggles, covering her mouth.

"Oh… Oh," I sighed. Students snickered and giggled.

"Ha, ha… he's dead!" Jezebel laughed hysterically.

"You took a picture of your departed cousin?" I asked.

"Yeah! He got shot in a drive-by," she said casually.

"Oh my God. I am sorry to hear that. My condolences. Why did you take this picture?" I asked.

Shrugging, "Oh… I don't know. I guess so I can remember him. I am going to add it to my shrine of dead friends and family on my locker door," Jezebel answered.

Candace Miller, an AP student who maintained a 4.0 GPA, glanced from her book and rolled her eyes, her daily habit in that class. I thought *how morbid* as Jezebel rushed around the classroom sharing her cousin's photo. The bell rang, and my students funneled out of the door. Candace straggled from the rear and she was the last to leave my room.

Candace began, "You know there was an accident on the freeway, and someone was decapitated, and the cops were trying to cover the body. Body parts were all over the freeway… Bystanders fumbled for their phones to take pictures as fast as they could. How sick is that?"

I reacted, "That's horrid. What is wrong with people?" *No respect for the living. No respect for the dead here.*

Candace continued, "After graduation, students have three choices. One, they have babies and go on welfare; two, they get locked up; or three, they die and are buried at Lion's Cemetery. Now, that's not much of a choice. I'm outta here when I graduate!" She turned and left abruptly. I never heard from Candace again after she graduated. I hope she got outta here.

Johnny Sacco threw pieces of potato chips at Jezebel's big Afro as they were writing an in-class essay. A chip landed and became lodged in Jez's hair. Then another whizzed by and the third one brushed her cheek. Jezebel whipped around, stood up, and started screaming at the top of her lungs.

"Please sit down, Jez and stop yelling," I said sternly. I gave the class a ten-minute quiet warning signal! "The first person to talk gets sent out on a referral!"

"Hell no! I'm gonna get that boy! Don't you touch me! Leave me alone!" she continued screaming. Jezebel was the first to talk! That was all I needed was for a student to provoke her. She demanded that I explain the purpose of the essay, and she accused me of grading her unfairly. I tried to get her to sit down and to start her essay. Then Jezebel threw a coin and it hit me in the face. She threatened to go home and shoot up her house!

She refused to stop talking and kept saying, "Hell no!" She wanted to go to the bathroom and declared that my class was a waste of time. Jezebel was unpredictable and volatile. She refused to stop ranting and spewed inflammatory remarks. I called the front office for security. Jezebel pulled out her phone and ran to the door as security opened it and escorted her to the detention room. "I'm gonna get you," she raved while wagging her finger at me. "This is a public school! Fuck you! You fucking bitch!"

Jezebel exploited my hearing loss like she did with her mother's blindness. My students were aware that I had an 85% decibel hearing loss, and I wore hearing aids. I missed about fifty percent of a conversation. I depended on lip reading and seeing their faces. Students like Jezebel made life more difficult. Jezebel constantly asked me to repeat myself, and she acted like she couldn't understand me. She challenged my teaching ability based on my hearing loss. She treated me like I was stupid.

I pointed at Jezebel and demanded, "Please, remove your earbuds!"

"Sorry, I can't hear you," she jibed, ignoring me. Without warning, she stood and screamed at an imaginary spider above her seat. She looked like Jack popping out of the box. She ran around the room, pushing other students, screaming. As abruptly as her antics erupted, it came to an end. Jezebel returned to her seat promptly unaware of her outburst. She quickly pulled out some papers for another class from her backpack like nothing happened.

"Put that away now!" I instructed in disbelief.

"I have more important things to do now!" Jezebel uttered defiantly.

The class just stared at her. She rested her pen, crossed her arms, and smiled as if to declare some sort of small victory. She tilted her head. We locked eyes. Tic tock. Unexpectedly, her phone rang out at full volume.

"Turn it off!" I demanded as I peered down at her with my hands on my hips.

Jezebel stood up, shaking her head no, marched toward the door, and answered the call. "You can't tell me what to do, I ain't no hoe! You fucking bitch! I gotta see what my Nigga wants!" She stepped into the hallway and continued the call.

I immediately grabbed my phone and called her mother from my classroom.

This was my sixth phone call to Delores regarding Jez's behavior. I told her mother that she is argumentative, blatantly disobedient, and disrespectful. She has used profanity, thrown objects, encouraged the class to mock me, and is aggressive toward others. She inappropriately asked another girl for a piece of her orange and made advances directed at her. The other girl punched her and pushed her away. Jezebel was confused and pursued.

Delores was speechless for a moment. "That doesn't sound like my dear Jez." She was in complete denial. I know I shouldn't have felt this way, but I couldn't wait to get Jez out of my class. We hung up. I turned around, and Manny had drawn a dick and tits on the board and was making stroking gestures! *Wonderful!* I thought.

Our administration made a point of parent contact by phone, email, or letter. I sent Delores a letter addressing her daughter's participation in class.

> *Dear Mrs. Lane,*
> *Thank you for your concern about Jezebel's grade in my English class.*
> *I have the following concerns:*
> *a) Jezebel's habitual lateness causes her to miss instruction & work. I need her to be in class on time every day. Valuable points are deducted from assignments turned in late.*

25

b) Jezebel is contemptuous. She uses the word "bitch" toward classmates and me. This is not acceptable.

c) Jezebel has thrown objects at my backside. It is very disrespectful, disruptive, and dangerous.

Please talk with her to let her know the seriousness of her behavior. Your daughter is bright and capable, but the behaviors causes problems.

Sincerely, Ms. Steinman

My last encounter with Jezebel was a few years after she graduated. I saw her riding a bicycle downtown. She was wearing super-size sunglasses with her hair in pigtails, thick makeup, and overall shorts. She was swinging her head side to side. I waved at her but she didn't see me and continued bicycling down the street.

CHAPTER 7
Delilah's Inferno

Delilah Swain was one angry student. She had a hard life. She is Black, dark-skinned, five-feet and five inches, slender, icy eyes, frizzy hair tied back in a bun, and a boat collar blouse with colorful wraps-yellow, orange, red around her waist, and flat shoes. A deep black scar zigzags down the right side of her forehead which has earned her the name Munster from her peers. She is a middle child of three. I had her older brother about five years before. Her father abandoned her when she was in third grade. Her mother is verbally abusive and is a manager at a dollar store near the school.

Delilah's Uncle Steve, who was addicted to pain killers visited her family late one evening. Delilah, her siblings, and her niece just finished eating beans and rice for dinner and were cleaning up. Her mother was hollering as Delilah dried the dishes. Her uncle entered their house slurring his words. He demanded to borrow money from her mother. Her mother refused his many attempts to sway her. Uncle Steve became combative. Her brother sat his infant daughter in a highchair. Familiar voices increased to shouting. Delilah became nervous, and her siblings continued with the chores.

Finally, Steve turned and grabbed the butcher knife and started swinging it in the air directing his anger at her mother. Delilah grabbed his wrist, and he brought the knife down carving a deep gash into her forehead. Blood dripped everywhere. Steve dropped the butcher knife and grabbed a rolling pin and beat her niece on her face until the baby went limp. Her brother leaped on him and attempted to disarm and sustain him, but Steve was stronger and pried him off before he ran out the door. Her mother screamed. Her little brother called 911. Her uncle reportedly had a gun, and as the police showed up, he sustained two alleged self-inflicted gunshot wounds to his head. I read about this tragedy in the news before I met Delilah. The three- month- old infant was DOA and Delilah went to the hospital and got 67 stitches. The family was never the same. Life changed for her after this. Delilah's life became intolerable. The family was emotionally and spiritually bankrupt. Delilah despised the world. She created problems at school, behaved aggressively, intimidated other students, and burst into emotional meltdowns. Her anger consumed her.

Delilah was involved in several physical altercations with other students causing injury. On the way to a rally, she jumped on Tina's back and pounded on her. Delilah ran screaming down the hall, tripping other students and jumping on them. Students were being held in the gym when she pulled the fire alarm. Pandemonium ensued when students crowded the exit doors. While running around the gym, she grabbed a bottle of soda from a student, shoved him, and stabbed another student with a pencil. Before the campus police could stop her, she instigated a verbal altercation with another student and attempted injury to yet another student. I don't remember ever seeing Delilah smile.

Once, she entered my class and purposely tripped Jean Sacchetti, who was walking toward her seat and made her fall down. While Lenny Tran was stretching his legs, he accidentally kicked Delilah's water bottle that was sitting on the floor. Delilah thought he did it intentionally. She picked up her pencil box and threw it at Lenny hitting him in the face. Both students stood up from their seats and began to kick and hit one another. Delilah punched Lenny in the face before I could call security to break up the fight.

In my class, Delilah ignored the no eating rule. She promenaded in with a muffin and shot me a taunting glance. I asked her to step outside with her food. She waved me off sassily and said, "Mmmm... Shut the fuck up!" I asked her to wait outside for security. Instead, she sat in the back of the class. Delilah immediately stood up and walked around the room. She paused at my pencil sharpener, toyed with it and then began to destroy it.

"Stop!"

CHAPTER 8
Is Our School Safe?

When I started my teaching career, I had high aspirations. I felt a lot of compassion for these impoverished kids knowing that much of their behavior was simply a symptom of their circumstances but struggled not to hate them because they tormented me all day every day. Leigh Valley High School had a reputation as one of the roughest in the district. When I told friends where I worked, they were dumbstruck. The district consisted of six large high schools. LVHS had notorious reputation for drugs and violence. Fifty percent of the district's special education students attend our school. The remaining fifty percent attend the other five high schools. LVH is well known for its brutal gang fights, lockdowns, vandalism, and behavioral students. The racial demographic is ninety-three percent non-white. All students are entitled to a free lunch. The graduation rate is seventy percent.

Teachers and students do not feel safe on campus. Security personnel monitored the buildings and grounds. Security cameras were mounted in the main hallways and parking lots. Most of the time, the cameras do not capture the student involved in the crime. When I park at school, I made sure my car windows were closed shut. Students were known to push lit cigarette butts through the cracked open window. The math teacher had a box of old music cassettes in the back seat of his car with a blanket covering them; a student smashed the window and stole the box. The tapes were worthless to the student. Some teachers even have extra car insurance against theft and vandalism on school property.

On the last day of school, we had a lockdown, and the SWAT team ushered us out. The police lined up on either side of the hallway with their rifles pointing down as they watched everyone exit out the front doors. They found a man walking down the street across from school with a gun. After several incidents, the school locked all the gates during the school day. The only entrance that remained unlocked during the day was the front office door.

Teachers have been injured and their safety jeopardized on-campus from slipping on a wet floor in the hallway to negligence of safety issues. During a rehearsal, the Drama teacher directed her students in the auditorium. The stage lights were not all working. She was giving directions while walking to the front stage. The center light burned out, so that area was dark. She could not see where the stage ended and stepped off the edge and crashed face forward into the cement floor below. She slipped into a three-month coma. Her students were frightened and didn't know what to do. It took a long time to summon help. The teachers argued at the following staff meeting that the school was not safe, and there are no protocols for emergencies!

Many incidents happen in or around our school that made us all safety conscious. The following occurred at LVHS.

A parent carrying an umbrella on her side came to check on her child's attendance. A man driving past thought that she was carrying a gun and notified police. Several units suddenly appeared from every direction with sirens blasting. They formed a semi-circle in the driveway facing the front door. They announced over their loudspeaker for her to stop, turn around, and raise her hands above her head. The police felt foolish when they realized the woman was carrying an umbrella!

During lunch, I walked across the quad toward the cafeteria. A student came up behind me and threw an orange the size of a softball at my shoulder blade. My neck jerked forward from the force. I had a large bruise across my back. Security radioed the nurse and administration. My students waited outside my classroom as the nurse examined me.

At our weekend football game, there was a gang-related homicide. Two brothers were shot; one died, and the other survived. Both brothers were former students. The administration promised us extra law enforcement on campus for a few days and told us the safety of our school is a top priority. Nobody believed them!

Mr. Green, emailed us that he received a call from Don Jones' mother informing him that Don might be coming to school with a weapon. The administration notified Principal Smith and the police. All school entrances were quickly manned to pick Don up when he arrived at school. Principal Smith spotted him at the front of the school before the first-period bell, and she walked him down the main hallway where he was handcuffed by police officers without incident. After being searched, Don did not have a gun. Later, a sawed-off rifle was found at his home.

Frequently, our surveillance cameras record unexpected suspicious visitors wandering around on campus. Early one morning, a woman walked into the office. She asked the office staff if she could see the principal. Principal Smith spoke with the woman who claimed she was a war veteran. She asked for money to buy a bus ticket. She said she served in Iraq, and her husband was dead.

Not only was the campus unsafe, but the building structure is over fifty years old and violates state safety building codes! We had asbestos, electrical shortages, and plumbing issues. The staff received numerous emails regarding these issues. Administration asked us not to make any repairs to any walls, ceilings, or floors. The building contained asbestos. Unauthorized alterations could lead to exposure. It was common knowledge that the main women's restroom had asbestos for ten years.

The water lines were filled with dirt from a repair. The plant manager and his team cleared the lines one area at a time. The Administration asked us to use a different restroom if a particular restroom was out of service. The emails were demeaning.

Teachers were warned not to have balloons floating in their classroom at night. The school had a few incidents of balloons activating alarms at night and on weekends. The fire and police departments responded and the district was financially responsible for the call.

CHAPTER 9
Administration Abomination

The administration staff was not who they portrayed themselves to be. Their duties included overseeing daily operations. They managed the faculty and staff, updated curriculum, secured funding for resources, worked directly with students and parents, and solved larger problems such as widespread behavioral issues of the students.

Our high school had many pitfalls regarding curriculum standards, school safety procedures, attendance requirements, and behavior problems. Compounding these issues was the root problem: administration corruption! Our faculty had witnessed among our leadership: relationship affairs, substance abuse, sexual harassment, discrimination, misappropriation of school funds, violations of campus rules, felonies, and suicide. It's difficult to work under leaders who disregarded their own guidelines.

Principal Smith, My Fair Lady!
The principal's ethics should set an example for the rest of the school. Our Principal Smith had been carrying on an adulteress affair with our vice principal of discipline, Mr. Warren. Talk about lack of discipline. They were both married to their prospective partners and had an ongoing romance for years. Many teachers and I myself had witnessed them gliding down the hallway resembling the king and queen of the prom.

Principal Smith's high heels clicked clacked on the linoleum floor as they entered the building with their dry-cleaning slung over their shoulders intimately enjoying each other's company. Their office was strewn dry cleaned clothes that hung from their coat rack along with the exercise machine in the meeting room. They really made themselves at home in our common space which led me to wonder, "What else goes on in here?"

A counselor confided in me that he knocked on Mr. Warren's door, walked in, and saw that Mr. Warren suddenly recoil from Mrs. Smith who was sitting on top of her desk. Our school enabled their philandering to continue on as long as it did.

The teachers were not the only ones aware of this relationship. My classroom overlooked the staff parking lot. During an interview activity, students mingled in pairs freely about the classroom. Something outside drew Johnny Sacco's attention. He stood waving his hands wildly calling the class to come look. As they crowded at the window, I called to them, "Class, get away from the window…sit down!"

Johnny would not budge and proclaimed, "Mrs. Smith is in a red car down there!"

The remaining seated students rushed to see what the commotion was about. "Oh, look! Mr. Warren is with her!" Snickering and whistling ensued.

"In your seats now! Away from the window," I ordered.

"Now!" I repeated. I approached the window signaling my students to veer away. Johnny stood on his toes, waving frantically down at Smith and Warren striving to get their attention. The students returned to their seats poking one another and sneering. I squinted down at the parking lot to see Principal Smith looking up at me from her car. I passively waved to her in an effort to conceal my surprise and disapproval. She reciprocated with a look of rebuke.

Shae asked, "Ms. Steinman… are they holding hands?"

The class continued to snicker, jumping up again. I lifted my hands up to stop them from returning to the window. Shae continued, "Ms. Steinman… everyone knows about Smith and Warren. Over the summer at the mall, I've seen them holding hands across the table in the food court."

"You did?" I blurted out.

"They didn't see me because they were so involved with their flirtation."

My student Tina piped in, "Yeah, Smith is married to an old man! Her husband looks like a mummy. I've seen him."

The class crowded tightly around me in attempt to pressure me to divulged privileged information but I had none. "I'm not adding to the rumor mill guys. I suggest you focus on graduating."

"Yeah," continued Tina, "That's what the other teachers said. They won't join our conversation. They look really flustered…They aren't fooling anyone."

Johnny snuck back to the window and exclaimed, "They are still down there!"

"Johnny step back from the window!" I shouted. The final bell drowned my voice and the students raced out the door.

Tedious Tango with My Fair Lady

"Knock, knock," I said as I stood outside Principal Smith's office.

"Why come in Ms. Steinman," Principal Smith replied casually while seated behind her desk. Without looking up from her paperwork, she inquired, "What can I do for you?"

"Did you get my email regarding Cash and how he bawled me out in front of my class today?"

Shifting her attention to me, Principal Smith looked up and folded her hands in front of her. "Yes, I did." She nodded.

"Did you talk to him?" I asked without breaking eye contact.

"No, but it is on my agenda for this afternoon. I will call him in during fifth period."

"Thank you. My student Kevin Reed refused to get off his cell phone as the class set about to read an assignment aloud. When I told him to put it away he asked me what I was going to do about it. I can't make him do anything. There is a no phone policy. I need some support here. I called security and Cash responded to remove him from the room. Instead, he decided to give a dissertation to my class that I was robbing Kevin of his right to a decent education by sending him to the office for possession of a phone. Cash yelled at me as I approached him. Some of my class laughed at me and the respectable students were too embarrassed to look at me. He was nose-to-nose with me and disparaged me as a teacher and a person in front of my class. Cash's assault was so unwarranted. I am beside myself."

"Do you have your rules posted Steinmac?" *(Steinmac was a handle that they called me derived from my school email address. It made me feel accepted).* She interrupted, changing the focus from Cash's tirade to my classroom procedures.

"Yes, I do and in more than one place! What can I do about these phones?" I asked feeling defeated, unheard, and alone.

"The students have phones, that being said, you have to think of creative ideas to incorporate these devices in the lesson plan."

I reached my threshold with her bureaucratic bottlenecking. "Impossible! I can't include a phone in every assignment. Should I take them away, or just ignore them? I have little to no authority in the classroom and absolutely no support from security. When the students don't listen, I resort to talking to a smiley face on the board. I'm outnumbered with a hostile group who are academic terrorists. When they defy my instructions, how can I preform my job?"

Principal Smith patronized me, "Well, you have to deal with it, Steinmac! Smart phones are everywhere!"

Unwilling to submit, I returned to my initial point, "It is not security's job to question the teacher's authority when a student is ejected from the class. Do I need to explain to you what Security's primary objective is? It's to remove unruly students and escort them to the detention. Am I mistaken? Am I?" I expounded.

"I will talk to him," she answered directly.

I reiterated my point, "I've seen Cash fraternize with our students. Security is supposed to underpin our staff's directive and keep the campus safe in a professional manner. They act as if these kids are their buddies. Our students need supervision not joy rides on the golf cart or an inside source for gossip. There is a big difference between being a friend and being friendly. I tell my students all the time that I am their teacher, not their friend."

"Okay, I will be sure to speak with Cash this afternoon," she promised.

"I hope you do and I'll have you know I informed our union reps that I was accosted by an employee. This isn't an anomalous event."

Principal Smith groaned as I left. She attempted to avoid the issue as best as she could but I was not the only teacher being affected by this. Cash chastised Mr. Devitis in social science later that same day. His student threw objects across the room, and Cash argued with Mr. Devitis in front of the student who was being expelled.

At the staff meeting, the union reps addressed the situation with our staff and emphasized this was ongoing melee.

"Good and Plenty" of Discipline

Mr. Green and Mr. Warren were our Vice Principals of Discipline. They both have intimidating statures, rugged features with militant haircuts. Mr. Green is Black and Mr. Warren is White.

These men together made a precision disciplinary team. They worked together in unison. Some teachers were afraid of Mr. Warren, but I was not. They dealt with the worst students at LVHS who were incarcerated or had severe behavioral problems. They contended with the toughest students in our school, specifically the ones who had gang affiliation. Nobody else wanted to grapple with these students, not even security. Together they performed numerous duties. When students had pending criminal issues, they processed their court hearings at the district or county level. They enrolled students in specialized state or county programs such as community service, vocational training, mental health, and substance recovery programs. Unlike security, these men were professional and effective. They had every teachers' back.

I met Mr. Warren shortly after he started working at LVHS. I needed information on how to process a field trip. His office secretary thought it was necessary to interrupt a meeting he was in with the administrators. Mr. Warren was agitated by my intrusion and assumed I came to challenge his authority. "I am the one in charge," he shouted while pointing at himself. "You have to go through me!" The counselors and administration who sat at the table were flabbergasted and gaped at me. I was astounded myself.

I said, "I understand that you're in charge and I am on your side. I only stopped by because I have questions about how to process the field trip forms. I heard you changed the procedure. Can we schedule a time that you can go over the new process with me?"

Mr. Warren replied, "So you came here for my help." His face became flustered and tried to conceal his embarrassment.

"That's correct. I just want to know what to do."

I excused myself and apologized for the intrusion.

Mr. Warren was tough but fair, and he always looked preoccupied. His demeanor was cordial and he made a point to greet the staff. He made hasty assumptions and rarely smiled.

Mr. Green was what I considered a ladies' man and was easily approachable. At parent meetings, he would pull out a chair for a student's mother and offered help with her coat before she left. He had distinguishing characteristics and was notably agreeable. His disarming manner was just as convincing as Mr. Warren.

I had a student once named Doug Terrel who stalked me. He wrote deranged and bigoted remarks in his journal and English essays indicating he wanted to shoot people. He was a troubled White student who talked about how much he hated everyone. His papers included a cornucopia of distasteful topics like murder, hate, suicide, and assault. He shouted out "asshole!" and other expletives during class. He carried toy guns and soldiers in his pocket. He refused to take off his sunglasses in class and wore all black clothes. Doug threatened to ruin my teacher evaluation. I sent him out, and he yelled, "Fuck you!" Then he kicked his desk and pulled out his lighter and proceeded to light his jacket sleeve on fire. The cotton fabric combusted and spread rapidly. In a split-second, his arm was engulfed in flames. Without thinking, I lunged towards Terrel tackling him to the floor with so much momentum that we tumbled into the desks knocking them aside. When we came to a rest, his sleeve was smoldering and charred down to the inner lining with a couple holes exposing burnt skin.

Mr. Green and Mr. Warren removed Doug from my class and suspended him. He came back a week later and instead of thanking me he continued to stalk me. My class was moved to a portable trailer with large rectangle windows. During lunch, Doug leaned against the wall outside and leered at me. My students couldn't help but notice. Everyone felt unnerved. This took place over the course of several days.

Lilly Pasquarelli, a recent transfer student asked, "Why's that boy standing there looking at us?"

I answered, "He is obviously stalking me."

Lilly suggested, "You aught a give Good n Plenty a rang-a-dangy and tidy this debacle up. You feel me, Steinmac?"

I couldn't have agreed more. I notified the office. Moments later, Mr. Green approached him, performed a search, spoke on his walkie talkie, and then escorted him by the arm toward the office. I heard later that Terrel had a plan do me harm. Mr. Green expelled him.

Mr. Green handled every situation accordingly. He made our faculty's job more manageable. Most of the staff were unaware that his position produced a tremendous amount of anxiety. His coping mechanism took the form of self-medication. Several nights a week, he rented a seedy hotel room for him and a hooker. One night, things did not go well for him, and it publicly impacted his position at our school. I arrived at school early and hopped out of my car unaware of what had taken place the night before.

"Did you hear the news about Mr. Green?" Mr. Jefferson, the science teacher, asked as I headed across the parking lot.

"No. What happened?" I stopped in my foot steps and turned toward him.

"Here, look at the paper." He handed me the paper with the front -page headline that read *High School VP Arrested.* "Mr. Green was at a hotel with a prostitute, and he phoned the manager complaining that the hooker stole his clothes and took off with his truck."

We approached the front entrance and intersected with some of our students.

"Steinmac!" called Eve. "Hear about Green?" she continued, eyes twinkling. "He got busted for coke," Eve snickered. A group of students from my English class were heading toward the cafeteria for breakfast.

James announced, "Hey, Mr. Green is in the paper."

"I saw it on the news," responded Delilah.

"He be fuckin' hoes and hitting the pipe hard son," ripped Manny.

"My dad always thought he was shady after they shook hands. Something about him wasn't right and he sensed it. He picks up on a person's vibrations. I guess he's whatcha call a Sensative," added Donna.

"It looks like that hoe-fo guilty as hell," rendered Jezebel. As her entourage continued towards the cafeteria.

Craig piped in, "My mom said I don't have to serve that Saturday school detention Mr. Green assigned!"

I thought to myself, *Great... What next?* We called them "Good and Plenty." Mr. Warren will have plenty of work to do without his partner's help if he is convicted.

Dan McGarvey was another student of mine. He was barely maintaining a D average in all of his studies. His mother had some legitimate concerns after she was called by the school to come pick up Dan. He was using his cell phone in my class. I confiscated it and told him to wait in the detention hall until the bell rang. He went to the office but became belligerent and walked out. Cash had to escort him back. Following this incident, his mother, Sheila requested that she be allowed to observe him in my class. And when she did, she was infuriated by what she witnessed and sent an e-mail to the administration. Sheila detailed the numerous disruptive students in the class. She wanted to know what the administration was planning to do with them. The admin, in turn, informed her that they would work with me to improve the situation and deal with those students as needed. Ms. McGarvey told them that I said I couldn't kick out special education students. The administration said that all the students are subjected to the same rules and policies as her son. She expected something to be done. Admittedly, I was anxious how this would be solved.

Before I headed to Mr. Warren's office, I stopped in the lounge for coffee. I saw a small group of teachers in a huddle whispering. When I got closer, I heard them gossiping about Mr. Green's incident in the newspaper.

Ms. Saeteurn defended, "He was a setup. This school is simply scandalous. If admins don't like you, you are as good as gone."

Ms. Fox, the counselor, ridiculed Green, "He has no self-discipline. He's a fraud. Fire his ass before he becomes a liability and sinks us all."

Ms. Gonzales, who teaches English, spoke softly, "I feel bad for him. He is exceptionally suited for his position and it would be devastating to lose him. Honestly, I liked the man."

Mr. Bailey sympathized, "Man, I could not do his job, not in this place. I get it. I would have lost my shit long ago if I carried his workload."

Ms. Staley, the Social Science teacher, added her twenty-twenty hindsight, "He should have called for a ride home, then reported it."

Mr. Bailey interjected, "Now that Mr. Green is gone, we are so fucked. I mean right up the swanker. No support. No Discipline. No can do."

Ms. Staley looked perplexed and replied, "What does that even mean?"

To which Mr. Bailey responded, "Aw nothing."

As I prepared my mug, I added, "I hope he has a Plan B to fall back on. I doubt he will be working in education again." Everyone glared at me, but they knew it was the truth. I saw Mr. Adams reading an article on the internet about Mr. Green, "PT Positions Replaces Administration Staff." The story was getting press everywhere.

Mr. McDowall asked, "Guess who the administrator is? Roy Smith, Principal Smith's husband!" Everyone in the group was shocked. Nepotism runs deep within the walls of administrative sanctum. The holiest of holies in Education.

Mrs. Smith's distorted voice muffled through the PA system in the lounge. She conceded that she did not have any new information about the situation and she expected us to handle this professionally in class.

I envisioned myself addressing my class. I would instruct them to avoid the subject. In turn, they hammer me for information. From that point, they will continue to derail the conversation away from the lesson plan.

The underlying truth is that teachers experience the same degree of stress as first responders. As a result, many teachers are prone to alcoholism or habitually smoke pot. Mr. Green was no different.

After he was charged, he was officially released from his position and no one had heard from him since. This event along with what happened next made me feel deflated. We lost one of the best VP's of Discipline our school has ever had. He was an extraordinary vice principle with extraordinarily destructive vices.

I stood outside of Mr. Warren's door, thinking about all this shit that came down. I collected my thoughts about what issues I wanted to address Mrs. McGarvey's visitation. I took a deep breath and knocked on his door.

"Come in," instructed Mr. Warren in his typical serious tone. I entered his office glancing up at the pair of deer antlers above his desk. "Well, good morning Ms. Steinman."

"Good morning, Mr. Warren."

"Yes, Dan McGarvey's mother visited your class and she sent me an email detailing her experience," he said.

"I'm sure she was not impressed. It was a difficult class, and the students were up to their hijinks," I said solemnly.

"Yes, it sounds like they were. We have an issue with her son that is going to require our attention. Listen to what she sent me."

> Dear Mr. Warren,
> My son Dan is a special needs student as you are aware. He has learning processing challenges. He loves his English class and his teacher. But there is an issue with Dan being able to learn efficiently and Ms. Steinman being able to teach him effectively. Dan said while Ms. Steinman is trying to teach there are a number of insubordinate students in his class making it impossible for him to learn.
>
> After coordinating with Ms. Steinman, I came into school and observed her English class. She had six disruptive students that displayed serious issues. They constantly interrupted, cross talked during lecture, used profanity, and essentially hijacked the lesson. They bullied Ms. Steinman.

They were angry, nasty, and violent and consumed fifty percent of the class time which is unfair to my son and the other students. Please let me know how I can help resolve this matter.

Sincerely,

Sheila McGarvey

Mr. Warren paused and looked up at me. The antlers on the wall loomed above his head like a crown. "That letter is accurate, Mr. Warren. It's true that most of the students do not want to be there. We could separate some of these best friend relationships to prevent them from feeding off each other," I recommended.

"You have to connect with your students. I suggest you talk to district personnel and have them visit your classroom to intervene," Mr. Warren advised. "Have you contacted all the parents?"

"Yes, I emailed and phoned their parents. If necessary, I call their parents directly in class while their kid is acting up. Some of them have real problems. The parents aren't always helpful. Delilah's mother came in and became so frustrated that she hit her in class. Latanya got between them but ultimately I had to intercede. I have tried other tactics like keeping them after class and lunch detention. These kids feel untouchable. They are failing and worse they are not even trying. Please do something Mr. Warren. I cannot keep my class from imploding much longer," I begged.

"We can't just move them! There aren't any more classes or electives to place them in. Every class is full to capacity. They have a right to quietly fail," he said sternly. Some teachers call him "Little Hitler" behind his back.

"They are far from quiet. Why can't you send them to the continuation school?" I pleaded, feeling desperate and already aware of the answer.

"There is no more room! In fact, there's a waiting list. Even the credit recovery classes are full! There are only so many computers and seats in a classroom," he snapped back. "We have to prepare these students for college readiness. You must control your class."

"You know as well as I that most of these students are not going to college. They should bring back vocational education," I said.

"Those days are over. All that matters now is completing core classes. Sorry, you have to keep your students engaged," Warren ended on a sarcastic note.

I thought, *this is going nowhere, and I still needed to discuss Delilah's mother coming for a visitation and observing my class. This district has tried so many different teaching methods, management strategies, and procedures. We had too many state educational code changes to testing, safety procedures, staff development, and mandated training.* My head was spinning.

I persisted, "I cannot even keep them off their phones. When I had that specialist from the district lead a group activity, the students listened to her, but when she left, I spiraled into disorder." Distracted by his large antlers, I asked, "Are you a hunter?"

"Yes," He replied.

"Oh, my partner is a hunter. He hunts deer," I said.

"I do not hunt animals," Mr. Warren replied.

"Oh," I said skeptically, "You don't hunt animals?" He shook his head seriously.

"What do you hunt?" I spoke slowly, feeling uncomfortable.

"I hunt teacher's incompetence." He clenched his teeth. *I pictured him lurching from his desk releasing an echoing roar just before he sinks his fangs into my face and rips it clear off.* I looked at him and smiled indicating that I got the punchline.

CHAPTER 10
A Teacher's Perspective

Ms. Lopez, James' counselor, was compelled to ask him, " Why didn't you enroll in seventh period when we discussed this before?"

James mutters back, "Man, I ain't got time for that shit, Yo. I've been hella busy. See what I am saying?" He unzips his backpack and shows her a hodgepodge of tattered books and crinkled papers. "And I play ball then," he added.

"You are behind seventy-one credits and you need to take a seventh period for this entire year. Which is more important basketball or graduating?"

James paused while he contemplated his options.

"You could also do an independent study to get the rest of the credits," she recommended.

"Are you smoking your own supply? No way. I don't want no seventh period. I want a zero period. Period!"

"Nonsense! We do not offer a zero period at this school like I explained."

James yelled out, "I want a zero period! You people should make exceptions to da rule. This school is all fucked up, Yo!"

Calmly, in a soothing tone, Ms. Lopez negotiated with this academic terrorist, "Okay, James, let's discuss alternative schools for you like credit recovery classes."

He stomped his foot, "Come on, Ms. Lopez. Just send me back to class!"

Ms. Lopez signed his pass without looking up, and James snatched it and stormed out. Ms. Lopez was relieved to be free of her albatross and checked her email. Her first email was from the school nurse.

Mr. Bailey asked me to inform everyone that he will be out
for a few days. Yesterday, while doing his regular home visit,

45

*he was attacked by a pet pit bull. He sustained bites to his
face, legs, and groin. He was in the emergency room overnight,
getting stitches and treatment.—Nurse Talia.*

Ms. Lopez was shaking her head, "Poor Mr. Bailey. I imagine we won't see him for a while, and I have to go over another disastrous student's home visit." She punched the keyboard and opened James' file to record the meeting.

"Knock. Knock," I said. I entered Ms. Lopez's cubicle office as I passed James on his way out. "How you doing? This place is driving me nuts. Counselor have been placing a disproportionate number of delinquent students in one class, and I forgot to tell you that I am having surgery and taking a month off."

Ms. Lopez stared at her computer screen attempting to fix James' schedule, which was a mess. She slid in her chair back and forth from laptop to printer. Her appearance suited her solemn expression. Sunken, dark eyes looked me up and down from behind thick framed glasses that matched the rest of her ensemble. She resembled Morticia Addams. "I feel absolutely despondent," I admitted.

"Are you getting depressed? You have been here a short time compared to some of the staff that has been here for decades. Have you considered transferring?"

"Oh, yes, but there are no openings at the other schools," I conceded.

Ms. Lopez leaned toward me in her chair and whispered, "Everyone here is under a lot of pressure. My husband does not want to listen to it anymore. I keep it to myself. Don't sweat the small stuff. And it's all small stuff. Trust me," she reassured me.

"That is why they all self-medicate."

Acting naïve, I asked, "Self-medicate?"

"Yes, meditate or medicate. You know?" She looked at the congregation of staff members in the office and pinched her fingers together in front of her puckered lips like she was smoking a fatty.

"Well, I do not drink anymore," I said softly.

Not all of them drink but many of them do," she confessed.

I asked, "Do you puff?"

She shook her head and whispered, "I don't partake but almost all of them do because they cannot deal with this place."

"What do you do then, Ms. Lopez?" I asked.

She motioned like she was drinking a shot and popping a pill. She smiled then dismissively pointed around her at everyone. "That's right. All of us have self-medicated." We both grin at each other.

"I came by to follow up on two things. First, I did some background checks on some of these students in my English class. Most of them never passed any core classes in junior high. How did they make it to high school?" I wondered.

"Students are not required to pass junior high; however, if they want a diploma, they have to pass all of their classes with a D, or they cannot graduate. They need two hundred and forty credits to graduate and must meet the minimum requirement in each area," Ms. Lopez answered, becoming serious.

"I don't get it. They get passed along through middle school and then enter high school with all F's. How do the admins expect them to pass their classes to receive their diploma without a foundation?" I asked, puzzled.

"It's unfair for the teachers and the students. It's nothing short of miraculous to get them by with a passing grade," she replied.

"Some do nothing at all. I have students who come in and just waste everyone's time or sleep in class," I said.

"That's right! They have a choice as long as they do not prevent you from implementing your lesson. Otherwise, you have to deal with them," she said firmly.

"That does not make sense! Some of them, clearly hate school and do not want to be here. They obviously want to incite mayhem."

"Well, just send them out," she commanded.

"My second issue is James. He is repeating junior English with me again while completing senior English. He does not do anything and follows the troublemakers," I explained.

"Oh yeah, James. He is seventy-one credits short of graduating and is a junior. James is in a position where he has to take a zero period, seventh period, summer school, and evening adult school if he wants to barely graduate in time. We have many seniors in this position who fail most classes in freshman and sophomore years and end up wondering how they are going to graduate in time when they are juniors," explained Ms. Lopez.

"That's a growing problem."

"Yes, and it is going to get worse. Failing students, poor attendance, and low-test scores are the biggest issues here," Ms. Lopez paused for a moment. "These issues are correlated. James has twenty pages of referrals. He has quite a record," Ms. Lopez rolled her eyes.

"Twenty referrals…," I began.

"No, no," I said twenty pages, Steinmac, not twenty referrals! Twenty pages on this guy!" Her voice raising an octave.

My jaw dropped in surprise. "Oh, oh, I see…"

"Yes, it looks like you are stuck. I am calling his mother after you leave. I have to, and you can call his mother too later this week." I realized the point was moot and I left. One student with hundreds of referrals. Damn, no wonder teachers are so burned out.

Ms. Lopez faced her desk, picked up the phone, and dialed James' mother. "Hi, Ms. Ward. This is Ms. Lopez from counseling from LVH."

"Hi."

"Yes, just letting you know that James is behind in all of his classes, and zero period is cancelled."

"I dropped him off before first period; I have no idea why he is not there?"

"Neither do I," replied Ms. Lopez. "He is not working on his research paper for his senior project. Instead, he chooses to waste time on the internet and complains that the research is just too difficult."

"I can help him get caught up at home on his research during the evening," Ms. Ward offered.

"Ms. Ward, James is at-risk for not graduating this year. We need to discuss how to help him graduate on time. It looks like James will have to enroll in a seventh-period class. His teachers are willing to help him every day at lunch. But James just makes up a lot of excuses."

After a moment of silence, "Oh, I see… when are you available again, Ms. Lopez?"

I followed my morning routine and visited the staff lounge before setting up my classroom. The lounge was busy with teachers gossiping, drinking coffee, checking their mailboxes, and making copies for their classes. Some teachers were so unaware of their surroundings as they vented about their students. I was listening as I checked my mailbox and grabbed a cup of coffee.

"Did you see how big those one-dollar donuts are?" asked Mr. McDowall.

"These kids are so fat that they can't even fit in their seats!" exclaimed Mr. Adams.

"And what about the clubs selling candies and cookies between the classes?" questioned Ms. Rosenberg.

"And they eat fast food. How can we justify that we are fighting obesity?" questioned Mr. Adams.

"I remember Nurse Talia had a seminar for obese youths. Apparently, the students were greatly offended," I added.

"They just have to quit selling that crap from the vending machines," advised Ms. Rosenberg.

We unanimously agreed. I rinsed my coffee cup, grabbed my stuff, and headed to my classroom.

The first-period bell rang and the *Pledge of Allegiance* was announced. "Everyone stand, please," I announced. Students sat with earphones on, kept talking, stared at the wall, or remained in their seats with their heads on their desks.

"Please have respect for the American flag or at least be quiet!" I continued.

James shuffled in a few minutes late, burping. James continued to burp and walked to his seat. He poked Amar with a pencil. Amar brushed his ear and glanced toward James, looking irritated.

"That was not necessary," I condemned.

"That wasn't necessary," he mimicked me. "I have to use the bathroom; it is an emergency."

"The first period just began. I cannot issue a pass for the first fifteen minutes, James. School just started, and you could have used it on the way in. Besides, today is the test," I explained patiently.

"Maybe you did not understand what I said? I said it is an emergency!" shouted James.

"I still cannot write you a pass!"

"What would you do if I walked out?"

"I will have to follow up, James," I warned.

Amar avoided eye contact with James. He was trying to hold himself together. I could see that he was nervous around him. James began walking around the room talking loudly.

"You looking at me?" James said, trying to make eye contact with Amar. "I will whip your white ass!"

"Sit down, James, and write the warm-up on the board before we begin today's lesson," I paused, and thought, *here we go again!*

"I can't see the board if I don't have my glasses with me, can I?" James deputed. It's convenient that he can see the board when he wants to.

"Take your seat in the front. I have never seen you wear glasses," I said.

Ignoring me, James said to Amar, "You, stupid fat fuck. Go back to wherever you flew your carpet in from."

Amar's face turned red.

James looked at me and replied, "He knows how I talk, and he does not mind. Matter of fact, I think Amar enjoys the attention."

I told him, "It's not okay to talk like that to anyone."

"I'm about ready to unload both barrels and you don't want any part of it. This conversation is over." James walked back to his seat, eyeing me, and grabbed his personal effects. "See, I'm getting my shit!"

"You stop being so disrespectful and rude to me," I demanded.

"You are completely wrong, Steinmac, others should be in trouble, and you… you… are wasting my time," James punched each word as he passed me. James maliciously whispered, "You have a nice day!" and he walked out.

"Where are you going?" I shouted after him.

"I'm leaving this school!"

I turned from the doorway and sat down at my desk alleviated.

Security later found him downstairs sitting at a table under the stairway, texting friends.

I checked my email.

Email from Detention Hall

Just a reminder, we notice that students are sent to detention hall in room F-1 with no referrals. Please advise students not to walk to F-1 by themselves. Contact Ms. Reinhart at ext. 2020 and she will send a campus monitor ASAP. Also, we have had students sitting in classes they do not belong in. Please call for a campus monitor to escort the student back to their scheduled class. Please e-mail the student's name to me. Thank you.

The Administration.

Well, at least a monitor was there when James left, I thought. I looked up, and standing in front of me was Christy, who failed my English class three years before.

"I wanted to know if I could talk to you?" asked Christy softly.

"Oh, sure," I replied.

"I want to know if I can change my grade. You know to do something to raise my GPA?" Christy continued.

You failed my class if I recall correctly, right?" I shot back and faced her.

"First semester, I got a B, and the second semester I failed."

"You missed too many classes," I reminded her.

"Yeah, I guess. My counselor told me to come talk to you about it," Christy said looking down.

"Who is your counselor?" I asked.

"Bryant… Mr. Bryant," she answered.

"And he expects me to change your grade?"

"I want to improve my GPA for scholarship opportunities," stammered Christy.

"And you're thinking about it now?"

"What can I do?" asked Christy.

I considered her options and said, "You better check out your English book from the bookroom… the third edition." Most teachers would have dismissed students like her and failed them without hesitation. But that only exacerbates the growing problem. Christy needed help not a lecture. And now she looked sincere about completing the work. I explained, "Read chapter nine and write an essay on what you learned. If you need help I can assign a tutor to you. Don't procrastinate. Keep focused so you can get the scholarship. I am pleased that you decided to take your education more seriously. Good luck Christy."

With a big grin she said, "Thank you Ms. Steinman. I will."

During my prep period, I stopped at the office to chat with her counselor. "Good morning Mr. Bryant," I greeted him as I entered his office.

"Hi," he said without looking up. One of our student's mother was sitting in a chair opposite his desk. "This is Mrs. Ward, James' mom checking in on his grades and credits." Mr. Bryant signaled me to wait a minute. He finished saying to Mrs. Ward. "We are putting James in the seventh period, which will begin on Monday. He will be with Mrs. Gates."

"I know that he needs to attend summer school and take another seventh period next year," Mrs. Ward confirmed while she handed him a form permitting James' class schedule change.

"He needs to drop his physical science class and be placed in advisory so he can make up his English nine and can graduate on time," Mr. Bryant explained. "James has been accused of bullying another student in the class. I met with James informally last week and had believed the problem was resolved. But I guess not…."

"In the future, please contact me directly," replied Mrs. Ward.

Our VP knocked on the door and entered the office. "Good Morning, Mrs. Ward. I took James out of one class where he has ongoing issues with the teacher involving bullying and harassing the other students. James must attend tutoring and has been warned of a five-day suspension if this or anything similar occurs again."

"Okay, I will see what I can do. If I could only control him." Mrs. Ward stood up and thanked the counselor and VP. She was grateful for their support. Mrs. Ward exited his office. The VP followed her.

"You know, Christy? How do you think we should allow her to make up the class if that is even possible three years after she failed it?" I asked.

Bryant looks up. "Oh… I assumed you had records from then."

"Unfortunately for her, I deleted them two years ago."

"Oh, I see," he said softly with a genuine inflection.

"She failed because she missed more than fifty percent of the semester. I would like to help her. These kids need more from us than the average student."

"Your students are lucky to have you. We appreciate your help on this situation," Mr. Bryant concluded.

Suddenly, a shriek echoed from the counselors' front office. A rancid stench wafted in from the hallway that overwhelmed our senses. We heard feet tromping across the rug, the door swung open, and people holding their noses ran out in the hall. Mr. Bryant and I dashed out his office into the counselors' front office. To our dismay, a donkey stood braying in front of the counter. Behind the donkey stood Ms. Saeteurn. She looked shocked. "I just wanted the kids to meet Beethoven! I did not expect him to take a dump!" she cried. There was a mound of steaming donkey shit in the middle of the office.

Ms. Saeteurn supervised the Music Club, which fundraised several thousand dollars for music students to go to Ashland, OR for the Shakespeare Festival. She said if they reached their goal, she will bring her donkey, Beethoven, to school. Regrettably, her donkey dropped a deuce the size of a football on the rug near Mrs. Johnson's office.

"What's the matter?" Mrs. Rosenberg asked. She backed out of the office from the smell.

Mr. Bryant and I stood there unsure what to do. Ms. Saeteurn could not leave her donkey. She had to stand next to Beethoven and endure his aromatic masterpiece.

In the hallway, I saw the counselors standing with their backs against the wall like the deuce was going to detonate. Students gathered at the stairs and pointed. The janitor mumbled with disdain as he set up a wet vacuum and a large bucket of suds to clean up the mess. Mrs. Johnson called Mrs. Smith and Mr. Warren, both of whom were at an administrative meeting at the district office across town. Mr. Warren screamed so loudly that Ms. Johnson held the phone away. This incident lead to a strict "No animals at school" policy.

While returning to my classroom, a familiar voice over the loudspeaker announced, "A clear dental retainer was found outside Principal Smith's Office. You can pick it up at the lost and found."

I chuckled, thinking, *Who the hell would want a retainer that was found on the floor?*

I passed Ms. Colfax's room, who was sitting at her desk. Beatrice Colfax sat, tears swelling in her eyes, holding a letter, and shaking like a leaf. I walked lightly and slowly toward her desk, eyeing her with compassion. She has been teaching at our school for forty-two years and was like a grandmother to everyone. She held a letter toward me, "Please read this for me. A letter to the VP." I gently pulled up a chair next to her and took the letter from her.

Her letter to the Vice Principal described an incident that recently happened when a student would not sit down. Cash was patrolling the hall when he heard the ruckus and entered the class room to see the student refusing to take his seat.

"You heard your teacher! She asked you to sit down," demanded Cash.

"I am sitting down," replied the student.

"Excuse me, you are not sitting down!" Cash approached him.

"You can't make me!" he shouted.

Cash reached for his walkie talkie, "Mr. Warren, please come upstairs to room two ten."

For once the class sat quietly with their undivided attention on the standoff.

Mr. Warren swiftly entered the room. "Sit down, or you will leave!"

"You can't make me!" the student braced himself for a take-down.

"But the police can!" replied Mr. Warren as he radios the campus police.

The cops arrived, hooked him by both arms between them and lead him down the hall.

The student yelled back, "I can't wait to get the fuck outta here!"

He finally got what he wanted and he hasn't been back.

I do not feel safe in my own classroom anymore," Beatrice admitted.

"God, Steinmac. In forty-two years here, I never had students treat me like this! When I came here, I was so green, and the kids were behaved."

"You are one of the best teachers, I've ever known, Bea. You cannot let these kids get to you." *Honestly, I couldn't even manage these students myself, let alone give advice.*

Upset still, Beatrice continued, "And look Mr. Warren got a death threat letter that he printed on the back." She flipped the paper over. It read:

> *Dear Staff,*
>
> *The administration has been investigating a death threat made toward Mr. Warren. It was written in the girl's bathroom in the main hallway. We take threats toward everyone very seriously. I realize that many of you have learned about this yesterday and were talking about it among our staff. However, be aware of your surroundings when discussing classroom incidents. Students have reported that they heard the discussions and are afraid to come to school and think there will be a shooting. There is no evidence about this threat. We will continue to investigate.*
>
> *When students hear this from an adult, they think it is*

more credible than from another student. If students approach you about this situation from Ms. Colfax's class, tell them there is no danger.

Thank you
Ms. Johnson, VP

"I bet the student I sent out with Mr. Warren, threatened him," sniffled Beatrice.

I stayed a few more minutes consoling Ms. Colfax until she settled down. Sometimes, we feel overwhelmed or have bad days. I felt empathy for Ms. Colfax. The students treat her like shit.

I headed to the library to pick up my workbooks for my Emerson lesson plan. Students were busy studying, using the computers, playing board games, and quietly chatting before class. As I made my way through the library to the bookroom some of my students were playing cards at the table when I overheard their conversation.

Yvonne Jones whispered, "Hey, Miss Steinman, you want my banana? My mom gave it to me, and I don't want it." She dealt the cards. A super-size banana sat in front of her.

"Sure, I'll take it," I answered. My stomach was growling. I walked to the table. Several students, Eliza Loomis, Ravi Patel, Jill Simms, and Tina Coleman, were sitting at a table finishing a project and goofing around. I left the banana on top of my bag at their table.

As I entered, I overheard Patti say, "Oh, no, I can't believe this." Patti was in charge of ordering new textbooks, barcoding, scanning, and distributing them to the students.

Our school was always short of textbooks and materials due to incorrectly filled out order forms or lack of funding.

Patti held her forehead in her hand, "I have been communicating with the district's Supervisor of Curriculum and who is in charge of all textbooks at the district level to resolve this textbook issue. I wrote a note to him telling him our VP of Curriculum here is a moron, and that she is pissing off everyone by constantly changing things, and she does not know what is going on. I actually replied and sent it to our VP, Mrs. Johnson, by accident."

"You are kidding me, right?" I asked Patti.

Mrs. J wrote back and said, "I am not a moron, and I will be happy to talk to you about your position!"

Both Patti and I covered our mouths as we stared at each other.

"Did you respond?" I asked.

"Yeah, I wrote back and told her I'll be glad to speak with you about my position, and I'm not apologizing! No way, I am tenured, and yeah… I will work anywhere else in the district. Just get me outta here…now!"

Patti was running her hands through her hair and waving them in the air. "Nobody can follow Mrs. Johnson, and we cannot keep up. Just get me out of here! Please do not tell anyone! I do not want rumors spreading around here. I cannot believe it…"

"Do you have my books ready?" I asked.

"I am not sure where those books are?" answered Patti. "We have six hundred more books to clear with the district."

I shrugged my shoulders and looked at her. "Okay, no worries. Just shoot me an email when you find them, and I will bring my class down here."

"Okay, Connie… Thank you!" Patti turned swiftly and began scanning books.

I left her room and returned to the table.

Don, a heavy-set Mexican student, is strumming my banana on the table. He grinned from ear to ear. "Here is your banana, Ms. Steinman."

Jill snatched the banana out of his hand. "Maybe it is too small for you, Don, or perhaps it is the right size? Oh, Ms. Steinman, Don said it is his size."

I took the banana and placed it next to my bag. It was a solid yellow banana when Yvonne gave it to me. Now, it had bruises on one side. Don returns, picks up my banana, and begins strumming it on the table again. "Ms. Steinman, it is shaped like his!" Jill sputters. The girls giggle covering their open mouths.

CHAPTER 11
Who Was Waldo?

Every year the administration assigned students to me who have failed multiple classes. These difficult students are emotionally exhausting. Most folks don't get harassed, assaulted, threatened, and stalked every day at their job. Imagine if the people you spent most of your day with, treated you like that. Now imagine being Deaf and trying to help people who don't seem to care about anything…

The second-period bell rang as the students quickly took their seats. Announcements blared over the PA system. Students silenced their phones and opened their books. Sunlight filled the room along with continual chatter. James nodded his head to his rap music through his headphones and slumped in his seat with a blank poker face. "Okay, James… headphones off," I motioned. James shrugged his shoulders and acted like he does not understand. James made no attempt to remove his headphones.

"This class is booooooooring," Eliza whispers as she pops a cookie in her mouth.

"No eating and no electronics," I instructed as James stared at me.

James leaned over toward Eliza pointing at Amar, "That fat boy up there gotta go!" She smirked.

"James, just stop," I demanded. He collapsed back in his seat and shrugged his shoulders.

Dan gaped at him. "What are you looking at? Don't you get it?"

I tightened my lips and gave James a disapproving look. "Today we are starting the Transcendentalism unit."

"Transgenderism?" joked James.

I ignored him. His friends BD, Eve, Manny, Jez, and Del were also in this junior English class during second period.

I begin, "We are going to start with Emerson and Thoreau. Then Dickenson and Douglas. After the Transcendental unit, we are moving into the civil disobedience unit, which includes our civil rights leaders like Martin Luther King, Jr. and Gandhi."

"I don't give a fuck about all those dead White people," mumbled Eve.

"Frederick Douglas and Martin Luther King Jr. are your people, James and Gandhi was Indian," I replied.

"So? They are not alive," he replied.

I rolled my eyes. "These people made a huge social impact James. I do not choose the subject matter, only on how I teach it," I sighed in exasperation.

Jezebel was sitting in the last row in the back, putting on her eye makeup. "Well, you better just get started so we can get this over with!"

"Well, Jezebel, this unit will take about a month. If we have a lot of disruptions, it will take longer. Learning is a day-by-day process."

She checked her makeup in her compact mirror. Then she lifted her textbook with both hands and slammed it on her desk. "Let us get started then," Jez announced after catching everyone's' attention

I scowled at Jez and cautioned her, "Last warning Jez."

Her eyes widened, "What!"

Delilah stifled her enjoyment in what was happening. Jez and Del were my two worst students in the class, and each was the other's enemies. I told the administrators that Del and Jez shouldn't be in the same class. I walked toward Jezebel, and she pulled a pencil from her pocket and began writing on her desk.

I scolded her like a petulant child, "You cannot write on your desks. You know that but you do it anyway. Explain yourself. That's school property not yours."

She replied with a smart-mouthed tone that made me want to hog tie and gag her, "Oh, really, is this destruction of school property?"

"Yes, it is! Please erase that now. These are new desks. What am I supposed to say to our administrators when they walk in here and see vulgarity on the new desks?" Jezebel silently mocked me while she slowly moseyed to the sink for soap. She pumped a handful of liquid soap in her hands and rubbed them together lathering her way up her forearms, past her elbows to the top of her biceps. She held her arms above her head and shook her hands, spraying soap bubbles all over. The row nearest to her ducked in their seats. Eve popped out of her seat and began to dance about smiling.

Things can quickly digress if a disorderly student is not immediately squelched from further intrusions. I had enough of their malarkey. A person can only take so much before they snap. I have taken more of their abuse then any individual should ever have to. I spun around and faced the class. In a low tone, I instructed the class, "Clean up! Sit down!" And they settled back down into the seats. It seemed the only thing these kids respond to is yelling. I started the lesson, "The Transcendentalists of the nineteenth century are today's quantum theorists. They pondered why are we here? What is the point of all of this? They were fascinated by nature's grandeur, and what it could teach us about the universe and ourselves. We will study Emerson and Thoreau, writers who felt in touch and in harmony with the eternal. Both writers were spiritual."

Eve sat back down next to James. Delilah and Manny were dozing off. They sat next to each other in the middle. I approached their seats and nudged them. They both sat up sleepily. I appreciated their effort to stay awake. For some, it may be a challenge.

"Class, open your books. Let's begin with Emerson's essay. This morning we will look at what the Transcendentalists believed and how it influenced what they wrote about."

James and Eve rolled their eyes. Jezebel dried off and took her seat. I glanced at Delilah. She was looking directly at me and rubbed her nose with her middle finger. I thought it was somewhat amusing the first time she pulled that passive-aggressive, Vulcan mind-fuck shit. At least, I was getting some sort of reaction from her.

While I looked right at her, Delilah sassed back, "What? I didn't do nothing!"

I turned toward the board. From my peripheral vision, I saw Delilah throw a paper ball at me. When I made eye contact, Delilah motioned that she is pulling a trigger, "Pop-pop!" She followed by asking, "What am I doing wrong?"

The problem here is multifaceted. First, if I keep writing referrals and sending students like Delilah out, I will never get anything done. Plus, it's an administrative nightmare and a no win for us all.

I continued my lecture. "The Transcendentalists were spiritual and believed that nature is sacred and that it was imperative to be connected with nature. They believed that everything in our world, even a drop of water was a microcosm of the universe. They saw God in nature. The Transcendentalists Movement's believed that the highest level of reality were the five senses and intuition was more important than thought. They were not an organized religion. They accepted these ideas as a way of understanding universal relationships. They defined truth as an ultimate reality that transcends what people can know through their senses. These associated thinkers formed a new club called The Transcendental Club which met in members' homes."

Manny's phone chimes in the middle of class. "Turn it off!" I demanded.

Manny took his time, exaggerating slow movements.

"A little faster, please! We are waiting!" I urged.

Manny responded nonchalantly, "Aww... don't mind me. Carry on."

I exhaled and stepped toward him. Manny refused, hiding his phone behind his back. He looked at me and shouted, "I don't give a fuck, and you can't do nothing!" Manny continued using profanity after I gave him redirection, he said, "Fuck, fuck, fuck!" Manny looks around, holding his phone tightly.

Next to him, Anthony is sitting, keenly focused on eating his BBQ potato chips. Manny leans over and grabs Anthony's chips. Anthony points at him and demands, "Give me back my chips! They are not yours! Steinmac, look!"

"Manny, just give his chips back!" I instructed loudly.

Manny played dumb, "I don't know what you are talking about!"

I lunged toward the phone to call the campus monitors and Manny bolted out the door. "Manny left class without permission! He is heading toward the large gym!"

Kiki and Cash cornered Manny and brought him back. Manny entered the classroom, sat in his seat, and thudded his head down loudly.

I stopped, glanced at the clock, and noticed that class was half over. I just finished giving a long-ass boring lecture about the Transcendentalists and nature. I wanted these kids to find their inspiration. My assignment involved writing a paragraph which described the characteristics of the Transcendentalist. I did not capture their interest. They continued to talk over me, turn their desks toward each other, rapping to music on their headphones, and slouching in their seats. Class was winding down. I was frustrated and angry. "Okay, class, let's stayed focused. Please write a paragraph defining the Transcendentalists' belief in your own words." The students groaned as Donna and BD quickly started on the assignment.

"Come on. You can do this!" I encouraged. "It is easy." But it wasn't for these kids. James had his headphones on, Manny was asleep, and Jezebel was still checking herself out in her compact. Donna and BD were the only two working.

James raised his hand. "Have you ever smoked weed, Steinmac? That is honoring nature." He is always steering me off topic.

"I do not indulge, James. How about answering the question?" Ignoring James, I continued, "Tomorrow, we start with Emerson's *Self-Reliance*, an essay that explores following your intuition, how there is a universal force that connects nature to all of us, and how to be present to reach your potential." Blank expressions stared back at me.

Donna Jackson glances around, shrugged her shoulders and says, "No one is listening, Steinmac, nor do they care." Donna finished writing.

Sadly, I glanced around. She was right. No one cared. I turned to the board to hide the defeated way I felt. I picked up a marker and drew a happy face and began speaking to it. I know that sounds crazy and perhaps pathetic but I was desperate. "Hello, I am Steinmac. Your name? Nice to meet you

Happy Face! Well, I have these assholes behind me that don't know shit about Emerson. Yeah I just said that," I said as I waved my hand pointing two fingers.

My students began laughing, nudging others to look at me while getting louder and ruder.

"She's fucking weird!" I heard Jezebel yell.

"Look, she is talking to a happy face on the board!" another shouted out.

"He's not talking back at her!" Manny said.

"Now, that's a Deaf White lady for you!" snapped James as he began loudly tapping his pencil on the desk. "Can you hear that?" James asked.

I cringed remembering those painful hearing tests I took as a young girl. Thinking about how the audiologist repeatedly asked me to say the word "ball" or "sit" to see if I could hear the right sound. I hated it! I hate being asked if I can hear something or not. If I hear you, I will respond.

I was trying to be funny to get their attention but nothing seemed to work. I felt hopeless and defeated. The bell rang. They all stomped out, crumpling their papers into balls, and throwing them in the garbage while letting their pencils roll off the desks. They just don't give a shit! They leave their pencils and trash on their desks or the floor. I stood there, crushed, tears welling my eyes as the last two students were about to exit my class.

Rusty, the valedictorian of his class, approached me with a tissue box and asked if I would be okay. Rus switched from a small, highly academic campus in our district to our school because he thought poor people were more authentic. I waited until he left. I pulled myself together and scurried to the teacher's lounge to get coffee during my break.

CHAPTER 12
Sick and Tired of This!

I barged into the teacher's lounge; my eyes still swollen from tears. Other teachers looked at me as I headed to the coffee pots along the counter next to the sink. Teachers were seated around the room, grading, preparing their materials, checking their mailboxes, munching on snacks, and gossiping. I grabbed my mug off of the hook and poured my coffee. I looked disheveled. Leaning against the counter, I quietly sought refuge in my cup. I glanced up and a flyer on the bulletin board caught my attention. It said:

Become a Leigh Valley High School Teacher!
We are recruiting diverse, energetic, and enthusiastic individuals with the goal of putting children first. If you are interested in becoming a teacher with LVH, please log onto our website and apply online at: www.leighvalleyhs.com

I thought, *I fucking hate this job.* I still had at least twenty more years to retirement. I stared at my steaming cup. Adele, who was in her in mid-twenties caught my eye. Sitting alone, she motioned for me to join her.

"You are having a hard time here? Huh?" she asked compassionately.

I bet all the boys in her classes have a crush on her. She is not much older than them and very pretty. She is half Asian and half White, slender, brown eyes, long brown hair, and always wears heels and a pencil skirt suit. Teaching comes easy for her. She offered me a Kleenex. I wiped my tears.

"Thank you. I am a lousy teacher! These kids do not want to be here, and they do not listen," I said with a sniffle.

"Most students only come for socialization. Most of them do like authority and they would rather be smoking weed and watching tv," she replied.

"No one listens to me. They ignore my instruction. I feel invisible. They refuse to do the assigned work. They taunt me. I had to call security six times today. These kids hate me," I confided.

"No, they do not hate you."

"Yes, they do! They have no respect and don't care about class."

"Most of them want to learn. Sure, there are a few who will not comply," Adele responded calmly.

"I just want out! I have no control! My ideas suck. I struggle with creativity. Trying to hear them makes me exhausted," I complained.

"You have to connect with them on some level, to attract their interest and gain their respect."

I explained what was occurring in class. "I could stand on my head and take my clothes off, and they would not even notice!"

"Tell me what happened," Adele replied. I explained what took place in the previous period and the ongoing issues over the past two weeks. The administration and a few lead teachers came into my class. I waited in the hall while they discussed appropriate behavior during class. The intervention created animosity and made the situation worse. I felt hopeless and defeated.

She asked me, "Do you have rules posted on a wall?"

"Well… no. I gave out a hand out at the beginning on the semester," I answered.

"That is not enough. They need to see it in front of them and you need to reinforce it every day."

So, we brainstormed ideas. "You have to connect the lesson plan to their everyday world, or they cannot relate," Adele continued.

"How can I do that?" I asked.

"Begin your lesson with warm-up question. Keep it simple like what is your favorite thing to eat? Gradually move to more complex questions that relate to the text book. Ask them to cite a specific example. Then have an exit ticket where they write what they have learned from the lesson. The aim is to teach them one thing each class session and get them to focus."

"That's an excellent suggestion. But how do I stop them from using their cell phones in class?"

"Have you ever taken their phones from them?" Adele asked.

"I have tried, but they refuse to hand them over. Then I send them out, and they come right back. Nothing changes."

"Post rules and enforce consequences," Adele said. She could see how frustrated and humiliated I felt. "Tell you what, Steinmac, why don't I come in tomorrow and observe for a while, and then if I feel I can jump in and give a lesson, maybe it will help you see what you can do. Okay?" she looked confident.

I realized she was right and what I was doing wasn't working. Her help was my last hope of turning things around. "Please. Tomorrow is perfect. Thank you." We agreed and then returned to our classrooms.

CHAPTER 13
Academic Transcendence

There are a handful of teachers whose classes are dumping grounds for students with behavioral disabilities. These students are one of the biggest issues facing public schools currently. Public schools must serve all students; however, private schools have the luxury of cherry-picking their students and are known for setting zero-tolerance policies for undesirable behavior. Until public schools find a solution for serving all students, including ones with disabilities, these kids will continue to fail in the *inclusion class*. Teachers, like myself, document our attempts to assist students with issues, sometimes with little to no results. Programs like NO Child Left Behind make this situation even more difficult to navigate through. The benefits of inclusion classes are arguable at best. From my experience, emotionally challenged students affect the students without disabilities.

The next morning, Adele entered my class and sat behind the students in the back of the room. I started with the warm-up describing the Transcendentalists. The students kept checking out Adele, especially the boys. They were glancing back there and raising their eyebrows, mouthing, "Wow." I heard a long soft whistle. "Okay, I need you to list five adjectives describing the characteristics of a Transcendentalist!"

"Who cares about this crap?" Delilah quipped.

"Yeah, why should we do this?" asked James.

I looked helpless. Adele jumped right in.

"First off, put your phones on silent and take your earbuds out and put it away," she announced. We were all surprised by her assertive instruction. The students followed exactly as she said. "You know the rules; same goes for Steinmac. We are both teaching this class now! Rules are rules for every class, and you will see them posted tomorrow!" Adele said as she glanced at me. "Now, for an activity to introduce you to the Romantic Unit. It is called Toe the Line."

The students cheered and some clapped. Adele took the masking tape from my desk and made a line stretching across the floor.

"Push your desk aside and line up on the tape facing the board," commanded Adele. "I am going to make statements, and if your answer is yes, you will take one step in front of the line. If your answer is no, then it is one step behind. If it is neutral, do not move. Any questions? No. Let's get started."

Everyone stood on the line, including myself.

Adele asked if they like rap music. Everyone took one step off the line. She asked if they like chilling out and watching television. Everyone took another step forward. Then she asked, "Do you live with both biological parents?" Half of the class stepped forward, and the other half stepped back.

Adele continued, "Do you have a stay at home parent?" Only a few students stepped forward. I noticed they were the kids that had more means and privilege.

"Do you have chores?" Again, about half the class stepped forward, and the other half stepped back.

"Does your family sit together for meals?" A few students step forward, and the rest took a step back.

Finally, she asked, "Does your family help you to set goals and support your effort to achieve them?" Only one student stepped forward.

Adele concluded, "Take a good look around, and what does this activity show you? Now, sit down and write a paragraph on what you learned."

They took their seats. Some stared at the floor.

A few wrote feverishly. The remaining students wrote a little, then paused and wrote some more. "Do not be ashamed," whispered Adele. "You have the ability to change."

At the end of class, Adele said, "On the back of your paper is your exit ticket. What is the point of this activity that we just completed? Write your answer and turn in your paper as you walk out."

The students quickly wrote their answers and crowded us with papers as they left. I skimmed over a couple papers and saw self-responsibility written another wrote self-reliance. To my surprise, I realized I actually had students who wanted to be here.

After they left, I asked Adele, "How did you do that?"

"You have to connect with them with something they can relate to like music, films, images, products, or ideas and bring it down to their level. You can relate the topic you are teaching to their living situation such as their family, home, environment, or sexual identity."

"I liked the questions you asked. I think I am starting to understand your approach," I replied.

"Many of our students are immigrants and come from inner city, low income, and single-parents. You have to research these students' profiles at the beginning of the year. Get to know their background and reach out to the parents. It will be worth it in the end," explained Adele.

"Sounds like a lot to do," I said.

"Just take a few at a time. Start with the most difficult ones. Have some games with get to know questions so they can talk. They love to talk. Establish five rules that are important to you with consequences and post them. You will be okay. Trust me."

"Thanks, I will!"

"Okay, I will check in with you tomorrow in the staff lounge."

Later during sixth-period assembly, I was thinking about my previous conversation with James' mother. I needed to contact her again.

Our school celebrates Spirit Day on April 20th. We wear costumes in honor of school pride. We had a school-wide assembly in the gymnasium during our last class. The theme was Hippie Day. I dressed in jeans with a long-sleeve striped blouse, a frayed leather vest with peace symbols sewn on it, layered beaded necklaces, a bandana for my head, and big round Lennon glasses. Many other teachers and students were dressed to the 1960's theme with mini-skirts, striped or psychedelic clothing, knee-high boots, jewelry, and long hair wigs. I brought home-made brownies. I asked a student, "You want a magic brownie?" This was probably the only school I could get away with saying that. This event made the school day livelier and pass quickly. Lots of students cut classes early on these days. The rallies consist of games, contests, and songs that support the school clubs and sports teams. Spirit day is a break from work for students and staff.

The last ten minutes before the day's final bell, students lined up to leave the gym before heading home. I saw James' crowd from my class waiting to leave.

"It is four twenty today, Steinmac!" shouted James.

"Four twenty!" said BD.

"Four twenty!" laughed Manny.

"Happy four twenty!" said Delilah.

"Do you know what four-twenty is, Steinmac?" Jezebel asked with sarcasm.

"I will be on the four twenty p.m. train, heading home," I announced with a smirk on my face.

The bell rang, and the students rushed off. Mr. McDowall was standing by the bleachers.

"You ready?" he asked.

I nodded my head, and we head off to his car in the parking lot. Mr. McDowall drove us to a cemetery near the school where we fire-up behind the mausoleum. Teachers always talk shop when we gather together off school grounds.

Mr. McDowall had something on his mind. "You know that girl who gives me a difficult time?" I nodded. "I suspended her for two days, and she returned after one. I told her that she owed me a day of in-class suspension in room F-1. Without a peep, she stormed out shattering a big window with her elbow. Security came running. And her family is responsible for paying for the repair. Mr. Warren expelled her." Mr. McDowall pulled into the cemetery and drove behind the mausoleum.

As he parked his car, I said, "You know Jezebel. She is habitually late and does what she wants to. Last week, Jezebel walked in with fast food. When I reminded her about no food in class, she walked right past me, muttering obscenities. I told her to step outside. I had no choice but to remove her."

Mr. McDowall listened as he searched his glove box and pulled out his pipe and a nick bag. He raised his eyebrows. "Sounds like she is a handful. This will help calm our nerves."

We got out of his car and sat down on the dry, freshly cut grass. McDowall began loading his pipe. He wore a dark, long-haired wig with a yellow bandana, a long-sleeved blouse with a low V-neck, and striped bell-bottom pants. We looked like we stepped out of Woodstock. "You know, I have Jezebel in the afternoon class, and I heard her threaten two students that she will whip their White asses! I reported her to Mr. Green. Nothing was done about it." He lit the pipe and inhaled deeply, letting out a plume of smoke and passed me the pipe. "Happy four twenty!" We smiled.

Before I inhaled, I said, "And she complains of having stomach pains and she tries to get a pass to the nurse or leave!" I inhaled slowly and passed the pipe back. I was starting to feel less tense. "Jezebel was loitering outside the bathroom. I stopped and she glanced at me and said, 'No, that's okay, I'll stand out here. My friends went to the bathroom together. I'm not into the group thing. You know what I mean?' I just looked at her and kept walking."

"These kids really have serious behavioral issues!" Mr. McDowall inhaled, tapped the pipe on the ground, and began loading a second bowl. "Savannah, a student whom you are lucky not to have, took my teacher's edition of the textbook off my desk to get the answers for her assignment! Savannah ignored my requests to put my book back. She responded, "I do not know how to label a drawing out of my book. I just need your book if you want me to properly label my assignment," Savannah continued, "If I can't use the teacher's text, then I will simply complete my assignment at your desk, Mr. McDowall!" Savannah threw her head back and snickered." He lit the second bowl and passed it.

Mr. McDowall continued, "Changing tactics, Savannah grabbed my pens out of the cup on my desk and refused to return them. She pointed her finger at me and yelled, 'I do not allow people to speak to me that way, and I refuse to discuss this matter until YOU change YOUR tone!' I gave her a two-day teacher suspension." I started coughing.

"These kids have emotional problems from family drama," I said. "If only people knew. "

Mr. McDowall took another hit and continued, "Savannah came to class on her first day of suspension. I told her she had a two-day suspension, and she did not belong here. She replied, "I am here now, and you need to mark me pres-zee-aunt." She insisted that I needed to count her attendance since she was in class and that one of the VPs said she had not been suspended. When I asked her which VP told her that, Savannah refused to say."

We looked at the cemetery view from the steps.

Mr. McDowall took another puff. The sun warmed our faces as we sat in silence looking across the cemetery. I took another toke and reflected.

"Some students have been downright abusive!" I said. "Phoebe entered my classroom. A student was leaning against the wall. "Nigger," she whispers and hits him on the back of the head forcefully on her way to her seat. She reached deep in her pocket and pulled out several coins and threw them one at a time at him." We both sat there in silence.

Mr. McDowall continued, "I showed a film in class. Yvonne enters after the bell rings and walks slowly around the entire room with a cookie and gets a napkin from the towel dispenser. I reminded her that there is no eating during class. Yvonne shrugged her shoulders and mumbled. James, who is also in this class, yelled, "No eating." Yvonne shouted back to him to shut the fuck up. James steps toward Yvonne. She kept repeating it as the verbal confrontation became louder. I asked both to sit down. Yvonne walked up to me and put her hand in my face and shouted she didn't like me. She slapped James hard across his face. He gripped his hands around her neck and choked her. "Get the fuck off me, you Nigga!" as she gasped for breath. I waited for security. All she got was two lunch detentions, and she missed both of them!" Mr. McDowall finished the pipe, tapped it, then gestured if

I wanted more. I shook my head. He shrugged and loaded one more. "I can't wait to retire, and I got twenty more years!"

"I have ten more, at least!" I answered. "Not only does discipline suck, but the protocols about progress reports suck too!"

His eyes were red. "The mid-progress reports need revising!"

"That's right!" I answered. "I have students who earn an A the first five weeks and then ghost for the rest of the quarter and end up passing because of this massive loophole!"

"The students know this too!" Mr. McDowall added while watching the clouds.

"Yeah, I had a situation last quarter. Cindy Collins had an A grade mid-quarter. I sensed she would ghost my class so I gave her a C on her progress report. She asked me why I gave her a C and I explained. She argued that it didn't make sense. Cindy went and complained to Mrs. Johnson, who met with me. Mrs. Johnson feels this situation turns the students against the teacher, and why do we do this. I told her it has been this way since before I worked here. Even Mrs. Evans, who processes grades and records, explained this to her. Mrs. Johnson keeps saying it didn't make sense."

Mr. McDowall offered me the last puff. I declined. I felt much better.

Mr. McDowall spoke, "Well, Mrs. Johnson is right. It doesn't make sense and it doesn't make the student accountable."

I added, "No one questions or tries to amend the district rules and protocols. That's why our district can't keep teachers here. The people above us don't want to create more work for themselves. It is easier to be complacent. I, on the other hand, am trying to hold them accountable. And I hope my lesson plan will help drive my point home. I want my students to look within and take an honest self-inventory and build from there."

"You got grit Steinmac. Not everyone has it in them. Some do but some never did. This place can destroy your passion from the constant assaults. But I can see you have made progress with your students. Looks like it's time to go. My wife is making dinner, and the kids are home. I'll take you to catch your 4:20 train." We headed to the station.

The train arrived on time. The yellow lights flashed signaling the passengers to open the door to exit. I ran up to the last car and pushed the button. Nothing happened. The man on the train pushed the button frantically. He quickly realized he was not getting off and he became irate. The doors on the other cars remained open.

I ran for the third car and boarded just in time as the doors closed and locked. I breathed a sigh of relief as the train headed for the next stop. The malfunction continued at the next stop. The doors opened in the third car, people boarded, then a handful of passengers ran to our car in a huff. I overheard them say, "The doors in the last car will not open." The people who didn't get off looked pissed! I realized that this has been happening for a while. I wondered if the passengers were trapped. How many stops did they miss?

Later that evening, I sipped the last of my beer and turned off my computer. I looked over my lesson plan and the information that I found on my students' profiles. I took note that James, Manny, Delilah, and Jezebel did not earn passing grades in junior high school. At this point, James and BD had a few C's and in the rest of their classes they had D's which was better than their peers. It was amazing they were allowed to attend high school. I planned to pay their counselor, Ms. Chan, a visit to find out how this happened. I smiled and closed my lesson plan book. I had an attention grabber, rules, entrance and exit tickets, and an activity to connect the theme to my students' lives. *I am ready as I'll ever be.*

CHAPTER 14
Nonconformity

I made minimal progress with the students in my English class. I needed to rethink my approach. Unconventional teaching methods were designed to give the students an in-depth exposure of the subject and to fill the learning experience with value. Methods used like role-playing, debates, and group discussion help reinforce the lesson. I combined a mishmash of techniques to reach my students with impressive results.

I hid in the back corner of my classroom with my back facing the class. Students entered the room and noisily took their seats as usual, not noticing that I was standing still in the corner behind my desk. I watched them looking around for me. The bell rang, I turned swiftly and marched to the front of the room. Their loud chatter abruptly stopped. I wore a black fedora hat with a burgundy feather poking from the band, a soft black cloak, a green blouse, and tweed pants. I carried a bag of lollipops that you suck on while waiting in line at the bank.

"Hello, Sherlock!" Rusty cried.

"Who's that?" asked Jezebel.

"Who the hell cares," answered Delilah.

"I told you all she's crazy!" shouted Jezebel.

"What's in the bag, Steinmac?" asked Donna.

"Hello," I addressed the class. "Today is a new day with a new beginning. Lollipops!" I trumpeted. Putting the bag on my podium, adjusting my fedora, I continued, "We will start with classroom policies."

"Policies, Steinmac?" Amanda asked.

"Rules, Amanda. This class definitely needs structure," Rusty answered, glancing at Amanda. He's so smart, Rusty could have skipped a grade and graduated early. Eve and Jez rolled their eyes, mouthing, "Whatever!" Delilah slouched in her seat. At least, I had the advanced students on my side. My quiet students Ananya and Ravi, lowered their heads and smiled. Certain cultures had more respect for authority figures, especially female students from India or Southeast Asia. They tried so hard to please their parents or other adults in their lives. These two always wanted to sit up front, and they seemed afraid of the African American students. I wanted my students to show respect to everyone and their differences. My students are unaware that I am a part of the Deaf community which has its own culture.

"I have five policies, and they each begin with the letter P," I asserted, turning toward the class as I picked up my whiteboard marker. "Let's see if you can guess and why? If you guess which one and say why it is a policy, then you get a sucker!"

Several students grinned, Delilah sat straight up, James leaned forward, and Manny put whatever he was twirling between his fingers away. Candy is king here. These kids are hungry. Some even skipped breakfast. I held my marker up to the board. They all started hollering out answers all at once! "Whoa, Whoa!" I shouted, lowering my hands with my palms faced down, gesturing them to stop. "Now, all this speaking out without raising your hand is related to one of the five P's. You must raise your hand. I am hard of hearing, almost deaf, and I can't hear what you are saying. So, one at a time. We raise hands here, and I call on you. No interrupting each other or crosstalk. Okay?"

Jez shrugs her shoulders, "Okay!" making faces.

"No, it is showing courtesy and respect for each other!" I explained. "Okay, the first one?"

Jezebel and Candace make faces at each other.

Donna raises her hand. I call on her. "Be Prompt!"

"Yes, and that means what?" I asked.

"Well, it is important to be on time!" she replied. I handed her a lollipop.

"Sucker!" whispered Delilah.

Donna glances at her, unwrapping the sucker and popped it in her mouth.

"Please, put your wrappers in the trash and not my floor!" I announced. "So important to be Punctual! So, people can count on you to be there! Okay, second?"

Amar raises his hand. I nod at him. "Bring everything you need with you to class!"

"Can you think of a P-word that says that?" I asked to encourage him.

He contemplated, "Pre… Prepared!" he stuttered.

"Great, Amar!" I gave him the sucker. He smiled broadly. We picked up the pace and continued.

"Polite. We gotta be nice to each other," shouted Johnny Sacco.

"True. You know why most people get fired from jobs? Not because they can't do the job, but they cannot get along!" I shouted. "You do not have to like other people, but you do need to be accepting of each other and learn how to work together. This is most important lesson that you learn from me!" I sensed an attitude shift. I could see I was starting to reach them. They were thinking.

We listed the last two policies, which were *productive* and *positive* including examples for each. I told them to break into small groups and work together to create a poster containing these five policies. The best poster and group will win candy. My students were excited about the direction the class was taking. We had thirty minutes before the bell. The groups finished their posters and posted them on the wall. I had them write an exit ticket listing the five P's before they left class.

The next day, I started my introduction to the Transcendentalists movement again. "Let's begin this unit again. I have an activity. Look at me. I am dressed like a Transcendentalists of the 19th century. I am Ralph Waldo Emerson. I love nature and believe everyone can pursue their dreams and achieve their potential."

"Dreams? Potential? We are hood kids, Steinmac! We are going nowhere!" James said.

Rusty turned to James. "Maybe, you are not, but I am. I want a basketball scholarship!"

James started to stand.

BD reached out and put his hand on James' shoulder and said, "Give her a chance; just sit down." James grimaced him and sat down.

"Think about the environment that these Transcendentalists enjoyed. Did it influence their writing? So today, we are going on a gallery walk right here in the classroom and evaluate photos of different environments," I explained.

Students were relaxed and looking at me. I had their full attention. "Before class, I posted photos of different environments in nature, our neighborhood, other cities, public places, etc. I will break you up into groups of six and will assign each group six photos. Each group member will have a notebook and pencil."

"Don't have a pencil!" shouted Jezebel.

"I will give you one! Each person will write about how that picture inspires them. How does the environment feel? What genre can take place there? Mystery, romance, comedy, poetry, drama and so forth. What kind of people would live there? Do you feel connected to something greater than yourself? Share your idea within your group. Then we will move to the next step. This is a gallery walk."

The students viewed the pictures and discussed how it would affect their writing. They compared nature versus inner-city life. They made self-discoveries. The activity affected them profoundly. In the last five minutes of class, their exit ticket listed one thing they discovered in the gallery walk. It was a much better class!

After school, I headed toward my monthly staff meeting in the cafeteria. I was eager to share my experience with Adele! I entered the staff meeting as the principal spoke with the staff. "The women's restroom in the main hall is being checked for the presence of asbestos. If found, that restroom will be completely renovated; hopefully, this summer!" The principal continued, "I'm letting you know, staff, that I am supplying every teacher with a box of pencils for the beginning of the school semester. No more students will be sent to F-1 without one!"

I scanned for an empty seat next to Adele on the aisle toward the front. I glanced at the principal and waved. "It was the best class ever, Adele! Thank you!" I whispered. She shushed me to be quiet and gave me a victorious smile.

The staff applauded while murmuring. "Second, this is not an overnight thing… teachers worry about how they will transport TV's, VCR's, and overheads to another room. Over the summer, we ordered and received carts to move those devices," continued Principal Smith.

Everyone applauded again.

Another worthless staff meeting!

The principal drilled on, "Please do not mark absent students in advance even if we know they do not show up. It screws up the attendance."

Mr. Williamson speaks up, "But it messes up my attendance with students on my scantron who do not show up!"

Ms. Lao whispers, "Who cares?"

Principal Smith instructed, "Do not mark students absent before they are absent. This creates problems with the state!"

Mr. Williamson shoots back, "But, I have to keep a separate list without the absent students as my list, so I don't get confused."

Ms. Lao leans toward me and whispers in my ear, "Get over it!" She smiles.

"Do not mark them absent!" Mrs. Smith shouts.

Mrs. Tate, the Special Education teacher, stands and bellows, "Hey everyone, I really work for the county. I have county kids, so my attendance is for the county!"

Mrs. Smith looks at her like she wished Mrs. Tate would be quiet, "That is nice."

Mrs. Tate did not notice the tone in Mrs. Smith's voice when she resumed, "So, I have lists, and I have to submit these lists to the county. The absences are so overstated that the state is giving me grief about it."

Ms. Lao heckled, "Who cares? Sit down!"

"The attendance is important!" announced Mrs. Tate.

"Thanks for sharing!" Mrs. Smith said intently.

Mr. Williamson asked, "What about the absences?"

Mrs. Smith repeated, "No one marks students absent unless they are absent that day!"

Ms. Lao, rolled her eyes, quite annoyed, "Get over it."

I chuckle and quickly cover my mouth like I coughed.

"One last announcement!" squeezed in Mrs. Smith. "The orchestra will be performing a concert of the year tomorrow at seven in the auditorium. Admission is free. Come and hear the improvement!"

Mrs. Tate heads to the back of the room, where a group of English teachers gathered in a semi-circle discussing "Back to School Night." Mrs. Tate rudely interrupts, "Now, don't be surprised if the students are so retarded that the rest of the family may be retarded also!" I guffawed loudly.

Ms. Saeteurn's face furrowed. She stares at Mrs. Tate, "That language is not alright, let's be respectful!"

Mrs. Tate snaps, "That's what I have been told to call them. Retarded!"

Ms. Lao pipes in, "Physically challenged!"

Principal Smith made one last announcement at the close of the meeting. "As your principal, I never thought that I would be saying this in a staff meeting. Please, when you are finished using the restroom, please check the seat and clean up after yourself. The seats are dirty. Thank you for your assistance with this issue."

The meeting adjourned, and I headed for home.

CHAPTER 15
Change Your Thoughts

The class finished the warm-up as I passed back the previous writing assignment. "Most of this class did an excellent job describing how to trust yourself and follow your intuition!"

The class applauded, which broke into cheering. The clamor caught the attention of Kiki and Cash who were patrolling the hallway just outside my classroom. I signaled them a dismissive wave as they pressed their faces against the narrow door pane.

"I am going to sit with each of you and go over your writing. Remember to "verbalize" your nouns. For example, in the sentence, I am going to bicycle to her house, change it to I am bicycling to her house. Or in a sentence, I am a skilled producer, director, and editor. Change this sentence by converting the nearest noun into a verb. Verbalizing your nouns to make what we say immediate and concise. Listen how I empower the noun by adding "ing" to make it into a verb. I am skilled at producing, directing, and editing. You can choose powerful verbs if you want!"

Donna raised her hand, "So we are writing our verbs to be present tense so the reader can see us in action at the moment?"

"That's right, Donna! And you choose empowering words instead of overused unimaginative words. There are a few overused verbs and adjectives like good, nice, okay. An extensive vocabulary helps you communicate effectively to others."

Amar raised his hand, "So you want us to read over your corrections and then type it up again?"

"Yes, that's right. Read it over and then write on your draft why I made those changes. Then go back to your computers." I pointed to their computer cart in the back of my room. "Make the corrections. Staple the corrected copy on top of the original and turn it in when you leave. Make sure your first and last name is in the top right corner. No name, no grade."

Donna giggled, "There is a town called No Name, Tennessee." No one laughed. Amar glanced at her and cringed.

"Better than Boring, Oregon!" shouted James. I have a pic on my phone of the exit sign. I tell my students from time to time that Boring is no place to be complacent.

Amar raises his hand and asks, "Is that town really boring?" The class rolls their eyes.

"You can always visit there and see for yourself! Any other questions? No? Good. You have until the end of class. Get started."

Amar helped me pass back papers while the students talked amongst themselves. "While I sit with you in groups of threes, the rest of you go over my comments and try to improve. I would like you to create a symbol or a picture of *trust in thyself*. What does it look like?"

I sat in James' small group first. I am impressed with his improvement. I told him I spent a long time on his paper and how much talent he had. We reread his paper from before the corrections and after. He heard and saw the difference. "See how strong you are academically? You can make a difference and take a stand intellectually with words instead of fists and a forked tongue."

My praise and time with him impacted James. He continued on making corrections as I worked with the others in his group. I told them that I appreciated the time and effort they spent on their assignment. They made corrections on their laptops and printed them. I met with all twenty-five of my students.

The bell rang and students stapled their new copy on top of the original, checking for their names, and handed it to me on their way out. James handed his papers to me and exited abruptly. "Have a good day," I said.

I arrived home later in the evening. I stacked the papers on the kitchen table, ate my salad, and dove into my papers. I was looking forward to reading my students' work. Most of the students made significant improvements with their writing and used empowering words. I enjoyed seeing their work and improvements. When I got to James' paper I saw the original one on top. Where was the new copy? The second page was exactly the same as the first. James reprinted the original copy. I spent a lot of time with him making his paper sound professional. He pretended he was making corrections, and he just reprinted the original. This is bullshit! I slapped my open hand against my desk. I brought up his profile on my laptop and found his mother's phone number. I checked the time. 11 p.m. *Too bad, I thought, I am going to call anyway. He deserves it and she is most likely home now!* I dialed the number. The phone rang twice.

"Hello," answered Miriam Ward.

"Hello, Ms. Ward. Sorry to call so late. This is Ms. Steinman. I am James' English teacher over at LVHS."

"It is okay. I just got home. Is everything okay?"

"I wanted to let you know that James has a talent for writing and if he takes academics more seriously, he would have more options to choose from and be able to graduate on time."

"Is he in trouble or giving you a hard time?" Mariam voice sounded concerned.

"He does have an attitude, but I am trying to work with him. I assigned a written exercise in class. James turned in his paper as if he completed the assignment, only to find out while grading them this evening that he had not done any of the work. James had plenty of time to complete his work. He really frustrated me because he tried to pull a fast one on me."

"Oh, Ms. Steinman… I am going to speak with him about this. I am sorry about his deceptive behavior and he will not be doing this again, I assure you. I am going to wake him up right now!"

I replied calmly, "I appreciate this, Ms. Ward.

"I'll pay you a visit and see if he tries this shit when I'm there."

"Sure, any time during second. Monday through Friday."

"Okay, thanks for calling me. I am glad you did. Call anytime."

"Okay, bye." I hung up. *Tomorrow should be interesting.*

The next day, I waited by the door. The first bell rang, and a few students entered. Donna was first, "How are the papers?" she asked. "Did everyone get an A?"

"All but one!" I said seriously. She looked at me.

"Who?"

"James... I called his mother last night!"

"He is in some serious trouble! His mother does not play around," warned Donna.

Students filed in and began to take their seats. Right before the bell rang, James enters humbly, looking down at the floor. Donna eyed him closely. James takes his seat, and everyone looked at him because he didn't have his headphones on. He looked troubled. The class became still.

"Well... James," I broke the silence.

"Yeah, I have my paper for you. My mother got me out of bed, chewed me out, and made me find the corrections you made, and do all of this last night. Here is the paper." He handed me his corrected paper stapled on the original.

I took his work. "I really appreciate this. I'm glad we both didn't waste our time."

"My mom was really angry. She was on your side and took away my headphones for a week until I show her what I am doing in all my classes."

"I really do care," I replied, "I can give you all the tools and advice, but I can't make you do the work. One of the messages that Emerson stressed is that you have to rely on yourself, develop self-discipline, and not let others interfere with your convictions, be an individual, do not follow the crowd, and be self-responsible."

"Yeah, my mom said the rest is up to me. She will support me until I graduate but if I don't, I am on my own. She said the choice is up to me."

"She is right, James," I whispered. "You have to make your own decisions now. You are responsible for your own learning." I turned to the class and addressed them, "You have the power to only change yourself, and that is your responsibility, no one else's. You always have a choice. Neither one has to be right or wrong; you have to live with the consequences with the one you choose. Emerson wants people to know their truths and to seek from within because you only know the answers for yourself."

"After I redid the assignment, I could understand why you like Emerson so much. He is inspiring," James said with a sincere tone.

"Okay, James, I will take your paper. From now on follow directions," I answered.

The class sat at attention. Donna and Rusty smiled at me.

"Are we ready to continue class?" Everyone nodded their heads. I noticed that Delilah, Jezebel, and Manny made long faces. Their resentment followed them like a shadow and seemed impossible to shake. Their families were dysfunctional. They needed to know someone cared about them graduating. The other students were excited to get to work in an environment without hostility. I was elated about my students' success.

"Write on your paper the quote I have up on the board and explain what it means to you in a short paragraph." I read the quote, "For every minute you are angry, you lose sixty seconds of happiness.—Ralph Waldo Emerson."

"Being angry is a waste of time!" exclaimed BD.

"Happiness is a choice!" Eve shouted.

"Stay in the moment," Delilah said.

"No, stay present, Delilah!" teased Jezebel eyeing Delilah.

"Write your answers down! Please begin now." I watched as they slowly got to work. Pencils scratched on papers. Erasers quietly rubbed out mistakes. Sentences turned into paragraphs. Ten minutes passed. "Time's up!" They put down their pencils. "Would anyone like to share what they wrote?" I asked.

"Don't waste your time being angry when you can be happy!" Donna shouted. She was Delilah's friend, an intelligent African American girl who wanted to join their little clique. She was too smart for this bunch and they refused to allow her in. Donna continued her comment, "Emerson encourages us to always try to be positive and put negativity aside."

The class stares at her.

"Brilliant," I complimented her. Manny looks at her like a lovesick pup. He is crushing hard on her more than ever. I walked past his seat and stood by the door as the bell rang, and the students handed in their paper before exiting.

CHAPTER 16
Connecting with Students

BD reads, "There is a time in every man's education when he arrives at the conviction that envy is ignorance; that imitation is suicide; that he must take himself for better for worse as his portion; that though the wide universe is full of good, no kernel of nourishing corn can come to him but through his toil bestowed on that plot of ground which is given to him to till…" BD surmises, "I think most people go along with the flow."

"Or believe in their secondhand thoughts," Donna piped.

"And you have to apply yourself!" added Amar.

"That's right, Amar. You can have all the resources, but if you do not make the best use of them, then they provide no help," I replied.

"James uses and abuses everything that surrounds him," accuses Jezebel. I sensed tension between them again.

"I don't listen to no one's opinion, especially yours Jezebel! I follow my own compass and do what I wanna do!" shouted James, staring Jezebel down.

"Aha, so what is Emerson implying about the person here in his excerpt?" I asked, trying to divert the argument from starting a fight.

Donna interrupts, "People should think for oneself rather than accepting other people's ideas. A person who relies on others' opinions lacks the creativity necessary to move ahead."

The class got quiet. At least, the argument came to a halt.

"That is right, Donna… don't conform and don't follow," James said.

"Yeah, right!" she replied.

BD continues, "In the first sentence, Emerson tells us to take action and get to work. My mom is always saying, 'BD plan your work, work your plan.' Emerson says jealousy is ignorance. What's the benefit of being jealous when it's self-defeating?"

"That's right, BD. And great usage of your power words. You are mostly unaware of what you truly want in your lives and think that a life of luxury and material will be fulfilling! But that's not true! Consequences come with self-responsibility," I said seriously.

"Self-responsibility?" James mumbled. He must have zoned out because he did not say a word for a while.

Delilah was not paying attention either. She looked through me like I don't exist. I asked her to focus. She starts digging in her backpack, opened a folder, and rummages through her papers. I said, "Put it away. We are waiting for you!" The entire class looked at her as the situation quickly spiraled into disorder.

She flips through her papers, walks to the garbage can, and says, "I need to shred some papers!" The entire class was in disbelief.

I shouted, "Not now!" She stood by the garbage can, ripping and shredding each paper into tiny, little pieces and throws each piece, one by one, into the waste basket. The class was mesmerized. I informed her, "You are wasting our time!"

Delilah focused on the trash and continued to rip up her papers. She tip-toed slowly back to her seat, smirking. She does not get why she lost her participation points in this class. *I cannot seem to get through to her!*

Delilah tried entangling Donna in crosstalk, but Donna pointed at me to divert her attention and focus. At first, Delilah resisted and grimaced at me. I continued the lesson, "Is sustainable self-reliance important for your development?" Delilah raised her hand, swinging her head from shoulder to shoulder. "Yes?"

"So, what's sustainable development?" Delilah asked.

"Good question. You, students, are the agents of change by setting goals to improve your life and others. Your development should meet the needs of the present without compromising the ability of future generations to meet their own needs."

Amar raised his fist and yells, "Independence! That is self-reliance!"

Delilah mimicked Amar in a high voice making exaggerated faces. "How does someone act independently, Amar?" I asked.

Amar glanced at Delilah nervously and answered, "A person acts independently when he has the ability to think and act without the help or influence of others or the ability to decide what one should be or do." Amar shook as a result of his disability and was self-conscience about it. "Dependency is the act of relying on others to make decisions for you," he finished. Amar is smart but his disability alienates him from socializing. It looked like an external source suddenly takes over his spirit when it struck. He continued, "Many of us are afraid to share our innermost thoughts in fear of backlash if we share our inner most thoughts. We are careful to choose our words." The class looked dumbstruck by Amar's answer.

Delilah snuck across the room and sat at another desk. She was driving me nuts! She pulled out work from another class and began to write. "Put it away, Delilah!" She ignored me.

"Turn off your hearing aids, close your eyes, and ignore me!" she lashed out without looking up. She rested her head face down on her desk and closed her eyes.

"Not possible!" I hollered back. It was challenging to teach these students with my hearing loss.

Delilah spouts out, "When are you going to raise my participation grade to one hundred percent for the week? Huh?" Jez and Manny snickered.

"Participation points are earned from the way you behave and how you contribute to this class," I answered calmly. Defiant, she cleared her desk of papers as they fell to the floor. I reached for the phone to call security and opened my desk drawer for a referral.

"Go ahead and send me out. I don't care!"

As I wrote the referral, Delilah ran across the room, grabbed the referral out of my hands, and read it to the class while dodging out of reach. "Delilah will not participate and keeps..." I reached for the referral, but she stepped back, and the phone cord kept me from stepping any farther. I demanded assistance and slammed the receiver down. Delilah skipped across the room mimicking me and other students. She kept hopping around the room. I just stood there.

Refusing to give it back until Kiki arrived. Delilah yelled, "You must be crazy!" After security escorted her out, Roman Petrashishin took the pink referral from my desk to see what I wrote. The entire class heard Delilah yell at the guard, "You're tripping!"

Ignoring the verbal argument between Delilah and the security guards, I announced that the class was almost over.

Amar raised his hand up. I nodded at him. "You know what, Steinmac?" Inquisitively, I raised my eyebrows. "Delilah is not very self-reliant!" The whole class busted out laughing.

"No, she is not! You are right!" The bell rang.

The next day, my students entered the classroom and took their seats. I had the warm-up question on the board. "What are your character strengths? Kind? Curious? Brave? Describe how you feel about your achievements. It is important not to sabotage your own efforts. Yesterday, we defined self-reliance. Today, we are going to look at ways of developing our own self-reliance. Please write as much as you can in five minutes."

Delilah rolled her eyes and sat in her assigned seat for once. "What does this crap have to do with self -reliance?" she snapped at me.

"You will see, just answer the question," I answered. After the time elapsed, I asked them to put down their pencils. "So, what are some of your strengths?"

"Kind," said Delilah.

"Generous," shouted Amar.

"Resilient," replied BD.

"That is a good one," I answered. "How? What do you do?"

"I take care of my mom," BD said, looking down at his desk.

"I am sorry, BD. I know that you are there for her," I answered softly.

BD nodded solemnly. "If you need to talk about her, we are here for you, BD. I can connect you with the student support center."

"I know, Steinmac! Thanks, anyway," BD replied.

"Okay, let's move on!" yelled Jezebel from the back. The students stared at me.

"Reviewing from yesterday in paragraph one, in *Self-Reliance*, what does Emerson mean by no kernel of corn can come to him but through hard work?" I asked.

Jez crossed her arms restlessly spoke, "Emerson means that each and every individual must pursue his or her own truth rather than seeking to follow the truth and ideas of others."

Jezebel is sharp but difficult at times. I asked, "What is the effect of this analogy in the text?"

"Emerson emphasizes that the work of each individual is unique to him or her," answered Donna.

"And he also connects the pursuit of individual truth with the idea of work," Donna quickly added.

"Of course, it is not easy for individuals to follow their intuition, but it is necessary," I ended.

"Can you define individualism again, Steinmac?" asked Amar.

"Yeah, Stupid!" quipped Jezebel. I gave her a warning look. She squeezed her face.

"Yes, Amar. No such thing as a stupid question." Jezebel was still making faces. "Individualism is defined by Emerson as a profound and unshakeable trust in one's intuition," I answered. "People are most content when they have put their heart into their own work and done their best. In other words, he stated that individuals are most happy when they pursue their own ideas, rather than following the others."

Eve blurted out, "How do you follow intuition?"

"It is your gut feeling when you get a hunch to do something or not," I replied.

BD read on, "The power which resides in him is new in nature, and no one but he knows what that is which he can do, nor does he know until he has tried. Not for nothing one face, one character, one fact makes such an impression on him and another none. This sculpture in the memory is not without pre- established harmony. The eye was placed where one ray should fall, that it might testify of that particular ray. We but half express ourselves and are ashamed of that divine idea which each of us represents. It may be safely trusted as proportionate and of good issues, so it be faithfully imparted, but God will not have his work made manifest by cowards. A man is relieved and gay when he has put his heart into his work and done his best; but what he has said or done otherwise shall give him no peace. It is a deliverance that does not deliver. In the attempt, his genius deserts him, no muse befriends; no invention, no hope. Well, Steinmac, many of us believe that nothing we have is valuable to share."

"This crap is so boring! It just goes on and on and on," Delilah plunked her head down on her desk. Jezebel laughed wickedly. Manny stretches and yawns. I wondered if I can ever fully get their attention. *I am not going to stop for these three until it gets disruptive.*

"So, why don't we pursue what we desire?" I asked.

"Because we are too afraid," answered Donna.

"And what is our biggest obstacle preventing us from obtaining our desires?" I questioned as I studied their faces. I had their undivided attention.

"Our self-doubt in our creativity," shouted James.

"Our minds!" shouted Amar.

Donna added, "You know, Emerson is telling us to stay true to what we believe in."

"There! Well said," I nodded and smiled.

BD sat there and nodded his head vigorously. "So, when you are brave enough to speak your mind and express your truth, there are other people who remain silent hoping that you or somebody like you will speak up first."

James adds, "The reason one person's, idea or statement stands out to another person is because that person is receptive to it… you know what I mean?"

Rusty read, "A person's eye looks where a ray of light is so that it can witness that ray of light. I think it means what we pay attention to in life."

94

Shae continued, "My parents are very religious, and they believe that God gives us what we need. People are gifted with their minds so that we can each bear witness to the world around us in our own way."

After BD rereads the first paragraph, I explained that this reading is only an excerpt, a tiny part of the entire essay. I told them the original is fifty long paragraphs. I continued, "The essay has three major divisions: the importance of self-reliance, self-reliance and the individual, and self-reliance and society. As a whole, it promotes self-reliance as an ideal, even a virtue, and contrasts it with various modes of dependence or conformity."

Eve shoots her hand straight up.

"Yes, Eve?"

"So, what does ideal, virtue, and various modes of dependence or conformity mean?"

I answered, "An ideal is a person's concept of what is right, a virtue is behavior showing a high moral standard." My students looked a little overwhelmed except for BD and Donna, who should be in advanced classes.

Amar focused on me while nodding his head intensely, "So Emerson believes that individualism and the ability to stand by one's own beliefs and be self-reliant is the most important thing."

"You got this, Amar!" I said.

"And what does this stuff got to do with us?" asked Eve.

"Not a damn thing," answered Tina.

"No… Emerson's essays do not just help you exist in the world. They urge you to make things happen and listen to your intuition," I answered.

Kirin, who never speaks up, asks, "How do you do that?"

"And why do anything, anyways!" Manny shouted.

"Shut up, Manny!" James shouted at Manny. The class gasped in surprise, even Delilah's head shot straight up. "Go on, Steinmac, how?" James finished. I was caught off guard and wondered if I could tame the alpha and then maybe I could reach the rest of them.

I continued, "Self-reliance tells us that the process of creating is its own reward. When we finally take steps toward our creativity, we can feel satisfaction! Emerson says that when we pour our hearts into our work and do our best, anything less will give us no peace." I glanced slowly around the room. I could see my students were in deep thought.

CHAPTER 17
Emerson Speaks

A few days later, in class, we discussed how Emerson related to us by following our passion, putting our best foot forward in everything we do, and not listening to others who discourage us. BD seemed desponded. I asked him, "BD, why do you look so far away? I thought you enjoyed Emerson. And you too James, Eve, Donna, Yvonne, Craig, Rusty, Amar, Ravi, Candace, and Kirin. Tell me you didn't."

"To tell you the truth, I feel stuck!" BD pounded his fist on his desk. "I am supposed to be graduating, and I only have enough credits to become a sophomore. My mother is slowly dying and it seems like I am the only one who cares. I do not come from a rich, privileged White family that takes all-inclusive, summer vacations. I wish I had hobbies besides getting stoned, but I am in survival mode. I wish I could go somewhere far away from poverty and profiling. A completely different life in a different place. It's got to be better anywhere than here." Everyone looked surprised at BD. He seldom shared his innermost thoughts.

"Well, I am White, and my parents are not rich!" shouted Fred.

"Yeah, me too!" chirped Don, who usually keeps to himself.

Rusty spoke up, "My family is White. They work hard and we are not rich. But they have always encouraged my sister and I to pursue our own interests and goals. I transferred from the high school across town for advanced students. I did not like it because those kids feel entitled. Apparently, it's a privilege to go there. I got sick of their snobby attitude!"

I added, "Yeah, Rusty is right! I had an interview at that campus before they offered me this position. I asked the principal there about disciplinary action. She said kids who get A's and B's don't cause much trouble and if they do there is a zero-tolerance policy. She explained that the highly academic kids don't want to be at the main high schools."

Amanda, who never participates asked, "So why did you take the position here?"

"I like diversity," I answered in a serious tone.

Shae shouted, "And you fit in here!"

After a good bout of laughter died down, Candace added, "You can change your life, now BD! I dig Steinmac's lesson on Emerson! The stuff she reads to us is for real!"

"Me too! You have to start from ground zero with what you got and move forward. Even small steps," added Donna.

Then all the quiet students Ananya, Kirin, Shae, and Amanda nodded in agreement.

"Donna is right!" I agreed. "You have to take action." BD looked up at me confused. I explained, "The greatest journey starts with a first step. Take that step! No one is going to do it for you." Everyone listened and BD kept his eyes on me.

"Look, I still need sixty credits to graduate! That is what I have! I am taking care of my mom, and that is where I am at. I cannot do anything!" BD yelled and pounded on the desk. He had our attention.

James spoke candidly, "Look, BD, before Ms. Steinman called my mom, I was still deficient seventy credits. I took seventh period, adult school at night, and there is a credit recovery class that Mr. McDowall teaches during third period. I am working really hard. In fact, I wish I did better earlier and I wouldn't be in this bind now!"

Rusty read from the text, "Trust thyself. Every heart vibrates to that iron string."

"What is Emerson talking about here?" I asked.

Donna raised her hand, "I think what he means is believe in yourself. Don't be swayed by others."

I added, "BD, you must have sound beliefs to live a life of integrity."

Dan asked, "What's integrity?"

James answered, "Truthfulness or reliability."

Donna continues, "Emerson wants you to be the best you can be."

I stopped momentarily and gave them a personal life example. "I recently chose to stop drinking. I felt I was wasting my time not getting anything done and hanging out when I could be exercising or getting personal projects done. I noticed when I stopped, my best drinking buddies no longer associated with me because they felt uncomfortable around me. To be concise, people are uncomfortable with themselves."

BD asked, "Can you explain what you said before about being truthful and responsible?" Everyone nodded in agreement.

I began, "You have to be honest with yourself and take an inventory of who and where you are! So, you only have half of your credits needed to graduate. Being responsible is action toward changing the situation. What can you do to empower yourself and move ahead?"

Candace yelled, "Take the GED and get the hell out of here!"

"True, one option," I answered. "Option two?"

"Do what I am doing now! Take an overloaded schedule- zero and seventh period, adult school, summer school, and credit recovery!" James added.

"Now, that's a full schedule!" I said. "And a lot of students here at school do not take responsibility for their own education. They do not do the homework, they do not come prepared for class, and they do not try to apply themselves! It is much easier to be lazy and blame others. Sure, maybe you live in a poor area or you have a disability. I understand! But you can overcome! I struggle to hear, but that does not stop me from learning and applying myself! I work hard to hear by looking at you. I put myself in a position to hear. I take the initiative to complete the tasks at hand and not make excuses for myself. I take pride. You have to apply yourself in your studies, obligations, and personal self!"

Donna, Rusty, and James stood up and clapped. I was surprised.

"Enroll in credit recovery, BD!" Donna exclaimed. "You can work at your own pace. Start with one class then start the second. You can borrow a laptop and work at home while you take care of your mom. It just depends on what you decide. It is your choice."

"Take the GED and just get out!" shouted Candace.

"Just drop out!" Dan shouted, laughing.

"It is a choice, not really an option, Dan. Not a whole lot of options to choose from if you do that. It depends on how much more time you want to stay here. If you pass the GED, you are done this year. If you choose credit recovery, maybe next year," I explained.

"I have to care for my mom!" BD answered. "I am going nowhere, never!"

"That is not true!" I shot back. "You can look into options for your mother like homecare resources, agencies, and state resources that assist her. Let us continue with Emerson's work and break it down! Maybe, you will find your answers."

Kirin Lal, who should be in AP English, spoke, "Vibrating on an iron string, communicates how one really holds on to their own opinions. Iron is a mineral that is known to be hard and difficult to bend. Emerson uses iron as the material for a heartstring; Emerson implies that the heart should be unyielding, meaning one must not bend to the opinions of others. It is the idea that one needs to stand by their own beliefs to be seen as a self-reliant individual. You have to make the right choices for you. BD, follow your heart!"

I felt so touched how my students connected with Emerson. His writing appealed to everyone.

I added, "When we are young, we act with independence and irresponsibility, and make judgments based on our limited experience. We do not think about consequences or interests. As we grow older, society teaches us to curb our thoughts and actions, seek the approval of others, and concern ourselves with names, reputations, and customs. What is maturity to most people, Emerson calls it conformity."

Rusty added, "It is hard to feel sure of ourselves, particularly as our personal failures accumulate. Yet, we have to be strong enough to follow through on our own convictions."

"What is a conviction?" asked Dan.

"Opinions," answered the class in unison.

James read, "To believe your own thought, to believe that what is true for you in your private heart is true for all… That is genius. Speak your latent conviction, and it shall be the universal sense; for the inmost in due time becomes the outmost. Tomorrow a stranger will say precisely what we have thought and felt all the time, and we shall be forced to take with shame our own opinion from another."

James placed his finger in the book where he left off and shut the cover.

Donna continued, "We are not rebellious, but the world can know us for who we are, and we can spend our time and efforts on reinforcing our character in our own way!"

I thought their critical thinking skills are superb! These students are college-bound and could teach my class. Everyone was listening and attentive; even Jezebel, Manny, Delilah, and Eve did not commit their usual distractions and interrupt me.

Rusty stood up. He continued, "We have to ask ourselves what are our wishes, dreams, fears, and hopes? We can be anything we want to be. Dreaming big and being it is not the same thing. It is how we consciously hold our beliefs in everything we do and how we challenge them. Some beliefs reside in every psyche in any society without these beliefs being the subject of explicit awareness. We have to actually be that person or have others believe you are that person is not the same thing."

I thought they are driving this essay home!

"Have you decided what you want, BD?" asked Craig.

"I do not know what I want except to get out of here!" exclaimed BD. He looked intense.

"Most people never think about what they want or even know what they want. I still question myself concerning what I want. The most important journey a person can make is the adventure of becoming self-reliant!" I addressed the class while looking intently at BD. "To become self-reliant, you must follow your intuition or inner voice! Most people imitate others and blindly follow. Self-knowledge guides each person toward their unique path. People should make decisions internally, not externally, or based on the opinions of others. Society is a barrier to self-reliance. According to Emerson, another barrier is the fear of our own consistency." I opened the textbook and read, "A reverence for our past act or word because the eyes of others have no other data for computing our orbit than our past acts, and we loath to disappoint them. Rather than act with a false consistency to a past memory, we must always live in the present. We must become, rather than simply be," I finished.

"We cannot keep living in the past!" shouted James. "I can see now how my attitude toward school in the past has persuaded others to see less in me than what I am. I cannot change the past, but I can take steps to change the future. If I continually beat myself up mentally about the past, then I cannot be present. If I stay present and change, then that creates a new future! I have to completely accept my current situation." The entire class looked at James. *I believe he has finally got it!*

Jezebel, who has not said a word during the entire class, shouted, "But nobody understands us!"

Donna yelled as she turned the page in her textbook, "Look, Jezebel, in paragraph eighteen, Emerson argues, A foolish consistency is the hobgoblin of little minds, adored by little statesmen and philosophers and divines. Then Emerson asks, is it so bad, then, to be misunderstood? Galileo was misunderstood and Socrates and Jesus, and Newton. To be great is to be misunderstood."

"So, what does he mean?" asked Jezebel.

"Self-reliance is a person's ability to listen and follow his or her inner wisdom!" answered Donna.

BD, leaning forward in his seat, added, "You know, I think it would help if I just got on a train and moved somewhere else where they do not know me and start over!"

"Emerson says that traveling is a fool's paradise. It is an idea that traveling offers what it cannot deliver! A colleague told me once that traveling is in the people, not the places. You cannot escape yourself," I lectured.

"Sounds like he has an answer for everything," said BD.

Eve, who has been listening intently, spoke up, "I will read the rest of this paragraph. Our first journey is discovering the indifference of places. At home, I dream of Naples, of Rome, I am intoxicated with beauty, and lose my sadness. I pack my trunk, embrace my friends, embark on the sea, and at last wake up in Naples, and there beside me is the stern fact, the sad self, unrelenting identical, that I fled from. I seek the Vatican and the palaces. I affect to be intoxicated with sights and suggestions, but I am not intoxicated. My giant goes with me where ever I go."

"Thank you, Eve! Will you explain what you just read? Emerson has a strong message here about being a self-reliant traveler. There is a positive and negative side of traveling," I said.

Eve gave us an excellent explanation. She concluded, "Emerson compares a person's expectations versus what actually happens when they travel. What realization do they have when their expectations do not come true?"

Everyone looks stunned by Eve's answer. The class is so quiet!

"A non-self-reliant person will lack a sense of fulfillment when traveling because their main idea of traveling is to escape the sadness of not being true to themselves. The giant in Emerson's excerpt typifies a person who is non-self-reliant whom cannot escape himself, no matter how far he may travel." I added, "A person traveling to lose their sadness will be disappointed! A fool's expectations cannot be satisfied!"

Eve continued, "Travelers are misguided. We cannot escape the void we feel if we do not have self-confidence! He says my giant goes with me wherever I go! We cannot avoid our problems."

"So, there are two kinds of traveling. What are they?" I asked.

"An inner and outer journey," answered Rusty.

"True, and you are self-reliant, or you are not self-reliant," I said. "A traveler who lacks self-reliance feels inadequate or disappointed. The person travels to escape their inner burdens or emotions and neglects their true self. They encounter the unexpected and the fear of getting lost or facing danger. The actual traveling is fleeting or a sense of satisfaction."

"But don't things get better if you start all over?" asked BD.

"The second kind of traveling can educate a person more about themselves, and the knowledge of their own individuality. This is an inner journey, BD! This inward journey is more important than physically traveling. One cannot achieve satisfaction while trying to please others!" I emphasized. Everyone was contemplating what I presented. "How can we become self-reliant? This could be your most important journey. How can you apply Emerson's teachings in your life? We all have to deal with our situations and challenges throughout our lives. What did you learn from all of this?" I asked.

"We should not focus on, copy, or judge others," answered Craig. "But we need to develop our own values and knowledge."

"Emerson supports the importance of the individual. Self-reliance is a person's ability to follow their own inner wisdom," added Shae.

BD leaned forward in his seat and exclaimed, "Allow a person to decide their own destiny to become who they want to be!"

"This class is fantastic! You guys are doing great! Society looks everywhere but within. My students, what we really need, can only be found within. Don't look outside yourself, seek within!"

CHAPTER 18
Depth of Life

It was late April, and it poured day after day after day. My students and everyone at school became depressed. Every day for six weeks, rain clouds thundered over the river dumping buckets of water over the city, and surrounding rivers were overflowing. In fact, the water was so high that it flooded over the bridges, the bicycling paths in parks behind the levees, and lower elevations within the city. The rain started in mid-March, and it rained until the first week of May. If you dared to walk over the bridge, you could look over the rail, and the water touched the bottom of the bridge. Entire trees were uprooted. Giant branches, dead animals, truck tires, garbage, shopping carts, and belongings from the homeless encampments rushed down the river in a big mass! They discouraged people from driving or walking across the bridge. The river could be heard from blocks away. The newscasters predicted two feet of rain above normal.

During the weather segment on the news, the newscaster kept saying, "Tomorrow rain, Thursday rain, the rest of the week rain." He did not foresee a break for a long time. People were worried. The homeless population moved inward. The sewers backed up and drowned animals and rodents floated in the streets. The river flooded over the embankments. If a levee broke, the city would have been declared a disaster area.

It was about 9:00 p.m. Tuesday night. Most of the city streets were underwater. The wind and rain came down sideways. People were advised to stay indoors by the emergency broadcast system. Only authorized emergency vehicles were allowed out. Two people could be seen walking over the bridge holding on to each other at the peak of the storm. The rain hit BD's face like icy daggers. He shielded his girlfriend Amy from the increasing wind with his coat. They walked back toward town over the pedway on the bridge. They both shouted over the turbulent river. BD was stoned. He was drinking liquor from a brown bag that he got off of Eve's older brother. His head was down as he drug his boot heels along the pavement. Amy pulled his hand as he lagged behind.

"Come on BD! I am soaked and cold!" Amy shouted. BD did not respond. Instead he let go of Amy's hand and turned towards the railing. The river was dark and raged furiously below. Without as much as a word, BD grabbed one of the bridge columns and hoisted himself up on to the rail. BD's feet adjusted and readjusted as he caught his balance. Amy's eyes widened when she saw BD.

"Stop! What are you doing? Get down now BD!" she demanded.

BD looked at her and smiled. He slowly released his grip from the support using his arms to shift his weight. A gust of wind challenged his ability to stand upright. He caught himself right as Amy lurched toward him to pull him off to safety. BD took several quick little steps along the rail adverting her attempt to pull him off. Amy's mouth was wide open. All of a sudden BD's fear seemed to drain from his body. He extended his arms out on each side and performed a worm dance with his arms. Amy screamed and covered her mouth.

A muffled voice from behind shouts, "Hey you! Get down from there! The cops are on the way! You cannot be up there!"

BD was caught off guard. For a split second, he lost his concentration and his boots frantically felt around for traction to rebalance himself. Water was rolling off the rail. His shoes slipped as he rotated his arms like pinwheels. His weight shifted and pulled him over the edge. Amy ran to the railing, never taking her eyes off of his face until he disappeared into the darkness. Amy was so shocked she didn't scream. She had never seen anyone die in front of her. Not to mention someone she loved. Amy's arms and open hands were stretched out over the rail as she heard BD shout her name just before impact. Amy stared down at the river wiping her eyes from the rain. She sobbed and shook uncontrollably.

At 10:20 p.m., I reached for the remote to turn off the news channel when an aerial image of the downtown bridge interrupted the normal broadcast. The road was barricaded by police cars as ambulances and firetrucks arrived at the scene. The newscaster reported that a teenage couple walked across the bridge disregarding the clearly posted signs prohibiting pedestrian traffic. A young man fell over the railing. The responders were unable to find him. The port authority was notified and was in route to dragnet the river. Flashing lights, thick fog, and torrential rain filled the screen. Silhouettes of rescue personnel stretched over the railing with spot lights shining down onto the churning water below. A close-up of Amy wrapped in a thermal blanket sat in the back of the ambulance while paramedics checked her vitals. She was shivering and in danger of going into shock. The camera zoomed out until the red and blue glow disappeared into the night. The correspondent signed off, "This is Dottie Otti with Action News reporting from high atop East Falls River Bridge." I clicked the remote and turned off the light. I laid in bed as the wind and rain pelted against the window. My thoughts drifted back to the bridge and Amy.

The next morning, I prepared for English classes placing the Emerson texts on my desk, writing the agenda on the board, and checking my email. Eve entered my classroom and stood behind me quietly as I wrote on my board. I turned my head and stopped writing when I saw her.

"Ms. Steinman, remember BD?" Eve asked.

I thought, *Why did she ask me this*. She looked out of sorts. "Yeah."

She said with a tremor in her voice, "He died last night."

"Oh, my God!" I gasped. I sat down at my desk. "What happened?"

"BD and Amy were walking across the downtown bridge. He tried to walk on the railing. Amy is not coming back. The police found her leaning over the rail hysterically calling for BD."

I covered my mouth with my hand. "I saw Amy on the news, but I had no idea the person she was with was BD," I said.

"They may not find him until the flooding recedes."

107

The second-period bell rang. Eve was already in her seat. I sat at my computer, staring at the email I just received from the nurse confirming BD's death. James, Manny, and Donna filed in quietly. James and Manny were expressionless, and Donna wiped her eyes with her bandana. They found out the terrible news.

"The port authority pulled a body out of the river, Ms. Steinman," said James.

"Was he BD?" I asked nervously.

"No, that other boy who drowned last week."

"They won't find him. He is out in the Delta by now," Manny whispered.

I did not know what to say. The rest of the class entered very solemnly. I knew they knew. Rusty and Craig came in with their heads down and slumped in their seats covering their faces with their arms. I walked between their desks and patted Rusty on the shoulder. The tardy bell rang, and the class sat quietly in their seats avoiding eye contact.

"I am so very sorry," I said softly.

James covered his face. Jezebel and Delilah walked in from the hallway insulting each other and shoving one another. They had no idea what happened.

"Yo James, what's up?" asked Jezebel. They both could tell something was wrong.

"Shut the fuck up!" screamed James.

Jez's eyes widen.

Rusty spoke up, "Didn't you hear?"

"Huh," both girls said simultaneously.

"BD died last night," whispered Rusty. They both stared at everyone slumped in their seats. This is the first time they both were expressionless and serious.

James mumbled, "Why would he play on a bridge rail? That sounds like suicide to me. He was working so hard to turn his life around. None of this makes sense."

Donna whispered, "He was pressured with school, his mother, and being poor."

"I thought he liked his life. He was smart, funny, and good-looking," added Manny.

"There is no answer to suicide," I said. "No one knows, and people do not think about those they leave behind and the aftermath."

James said, "Think I'm gonna give up drinking and smoking. The party is over. How am I supposed enjoy that shit without my boy?"

Rusty said, "You should James. You're better than that. Don't waste your natural talents."

Eve responded, "Of all people, why BD? What does Emerson say about death, Ms. Steinman?"

"He thought about immediacy, intuition, lack of dependence on the past, and closeness to nature. He questions human wholeness. Emerson mastered nature through the all-powerful and all-trusting self. He found his higher power and felt that a divine source is in everything."

"BD's mother is very religious, and this did not do him any good!" James said.

"This is what happens when you grow up in the hood. We have more to worry about than just a stray bullet," warned Manny.

"Yeah, that is the truth!" answered Delilah. Everyone gestured her to shut up. She did not seem affected at all.

"His mother loved him so much. She must be devastated. I wish I knew what he was going through. Perhaps I could have helped. I feel terrible," said Eve.

"Emerson's *Self-Reliance* essay is a warning," interrupted James. "Our lives can end unexpectedly by our own carelessness. But knowing that changes nothing."

"Untrue, James. When we act upon self-evident truths then we cause profound change. But we can start with small steps right now like bringing a pencil to class every day," I answered. "Emerson feels that we need to listen to the spirit within us."

Manny exclaimed, "BD, felt like no one listened to him. He seemed disconnected, and he was distancing himself from others. I think Emerson's purpose was to achieve oneness between self and the rest of creation, assuring a symbiotic harmony. You know what I'm mean, Yo?"

"I think that was the smartest thing you've ever said, Manny. Well done," I praised.

"We cannot forget BD! We have to do something for him!" James' voice quivered.

"What can we do to memorialize him?" Donna asked.

"We can raise funds for a plaque in his honor where he fell," said Jezebel.

"That's right. We could pass a donation hat to collect funds between classes and at lunch," Delilah added.

"Good idea," I said.

"I could write a memorial for the graduation," sniffled James.

"We need to buy candles, flowers, and small things that he liked and place a vigil under the plaque," Tina added.

"We need to buy flowers and a card for his mother. Perhaps, we can go as a class and extend our sincerest condolences," I suggested.

Jean added, "We can make a page just for him in the yearbook. He won't be forgotten."

"I could have done something," cried James.

"I feel the same way. I think we all do," I said.

CHAPTER 19
Graduation

James stood in front of me a week before graduation. Eve and Manny headed out of my room to the cafeteria. It was nothing short of miraculous that James was finally graduating after cutting so many days, nineteen pages of referrals, hundreds of phone calls home, dozens of parent conferences, and had marijuana confiscated more times than anyone in juvenile hall. His smile was contagious. He pulled apart the plastic bag containing his cap and gown. "Ah," he repeated. He pulled out the contents and let the bag float to the floor. Excitedly, James put his robe on and zipped it up and adjusted his tassel. "Hey, Steinmac, I am the first generation to graduate high school!"

"I knew you could do it. I am so very impressed. I have taught a lot of students James. But you and your friends have taught me something too. Perseverance." I glanced down at the floor a moment, looked at him again, thinking, *I have never seen this boy smile so wildly*. At that moment, it all hit me. I turned away from him with a lump in my throat. I inhaled a deep breath and regained my composure.

"You are a special teacher. Thank you for not giving up on me or our class. We took advantage of your kindness and exhausted your patience. I feel terrible for the difficulty we caused in class. You did not deserve that. My family and I are grateful. I will never forget what you taught us. I am going to miss you Ms. Connie Steinman. Who is going to inspire us now?" James reached out for a hug. I pulled him in and wrapped my arms around him.

"You are welcome James. It wasn't easy but it was well worth it. I consider you all my kids." I let go, looked James in the eyes and thought how much he has changed. He took off his hat and picked up the plastic bag from the floor. "See you later. Gotta get my free lunch. Ain't many of them in life. You know what I'm saying?"

I smiled and watched him leave. I sat at my desk and checked my staff email. I opened an email from Adele and was surprised to read the letter to Mrs. Smith.

Dear Principal Smith,

Please accept this letter as my formal resignation.

You made an offensive comment at a meeting held between the district and teachers. You stated that many of the teachers who leave LVH use their experience here to hone their craft before leaving for more desirable schools. I want to make it clear, that is not the motivation behind my departure. You are the reason.

This week I signed a contract for an English position in a different district. I am excited to begin working for a principal with a clear vision and who fosters creativity amongst his staff.

For five years, the Athletics Department has guided me on this journey as a coach and mentor to numerous aspiring student-athletes. Each and every coach and teacher go above and beyond their contractual obligations. These individuals are solely responsible for developing a sense of personal responsibility and self-value in countless Bison athletes. The English Department has asked me to think critically about my own teaching practices and fostered creative lesson planning. The teachers I have met in this department helped me to grow and become the teacher I am today. I am forever grateful for their passion, empathy, and support. They are a rare and inspiring group.

So, it is with a clear conscience and heavy heart that I say goodbye to Leigh Valley High School. I will miss the staff

and students dearly. Please love them as I have for the past
five years and will continue to do from afar. I have attached
a copy of this email to coincide with the official district form.
Good luck with the upcoming school year.

Adele Beaumont, English Dept.

I was overwhelmed with emotion. Another gifted teacher had left due to administrative blunders and district procedures.

In mid-June, James' graduating class sat in the downtown auditorium with their families and friends. The superintendent, administration, and teachers sat in a line horizontally across the stage with flowers behind them. The US flag was positioned on the right side of the podium. The valedictorians were seated at center stage. James and several other students were selected to speak. James was handling the memorial honoring his friend. He rung his hands nervously. I stood with the other teachers supervising students as they stepped onto the stage to receive their diploma and shake hands with administration. I smiled at James reassuringly. He nodded his head.

The last valedictorian spoke, "Raise your hand if at some point, you or your teachers doubted you were going to graduate? I want to congratulate you all. We defeated the stereotype and the naysayer. Some did not believe they would make it, but we did, and no one can take that from us. Many of us will go onto college and others into the workforce or service. What we learned in high school wasn't only from the textbooks but also from each other. We learned to embrace our talents as well as our differences. Together we made these past four years the most special time of our lives. We will take our experiences with us that will shape our world. Tragically, a few of us aren't here today. I would like to take a moment of silence for the fallen few." Everyone bowed their heads. After an extended moment, she concluded, "Thank you. Congratulations class!" she stopped and sat down. The audience roared with applause.

James was introduced as the audience continued to applaud. He stood at the podium. "Hi. I'm James. Today we celebrate our completion of high school and celebrate the life of one of our fellow students. When someone loses all hope and takes their own life, many questions remain unanswered. What could I have done? How could I have helped? Why did he see no other choice?

BD was my closest friend. He should be here sitting between Manny and Jezebel, graduating, and thinking about the future. My condolences to his family. Most people who knew him did not know he suffered from depression. He hid his darkness behind his laughter. BD was the funniest person I have ever met. He would have me busting up so bad that I'd be gasping for air. He always saw the humor in any situation. He had compassion for those who needed help. He would do anything for his friends and family. BD loved punk rock, skateboarding, blazing up, his mama, and his buds. I'm not sure what I'll do without you bro. I think a quote from Emerson captures my sentiment best, "It is not the length of life but the depth of life." I know I will never see you again, my friend. I don't know why your time had to be cut short, but I am grateful to have had you in my life. The time we spent together behind the wall, I will recant with fondest of memories. May you finally find the peace you could not while you were here. We'll never forget... Thank you."

James exited the stage. As he approached the teachers standing off stage, he stopped and looked at me, and smiled. I placed my hand on his shoulder. "That was a lovely memorial. I will never forget him either." I quoted Emerson one final time, "The purpose of life is not just to be happy. It is to be useful, to be honorable, to be compassionate, and to have it make some difference that you have lived and lived well." I reached out to hug James, and he hugged me back.

"Thank you, Ms. Steinman. Thank you for not giving up on our class. You were the best teacher I ever had."

"You're welcome, James. Good luck."

I watched him rejoin his class. Principal Smith dismissed the students and staff. As everyone filed out of the auditorium, I could see James' yellow headphones disappear into the crowd. That's when it hit me! I finally broke through his wall!

POSTFACE
The Outlands

Welcome to Sacramento, California! In the early 1900s, neighborhoods on the Southside of the city began to thrive! The homes that were built were small compared to today's standards. It was a rural town that was considered a central center with affordable housing, lucrative businesses, and lots of entertainment. It developed its own small downtown, which successfully met the day-to-day needs of its residents. In form and function, it exemplified many of today's "smart growth" principles. The streets and sidewalks were narrow. The grass area between the street and sidewalk were lined up with oak trees and palm trees. Each home had a two to a three-acre yard; some yards were an empty grass field or cultivated into a vegetable garden with fruit trees. This area was nicknamed "City of Trees." This area was home to the state fair and constructed its first streetcar, which connected this area to the downtown area. It even had an amusement park!

Married couples were buying homes and starting their families. Most families worked on farms, canning factories in the west end of the city, the military base, or in the town's local businesses. Many residents worked for the Southern Pacific Rail Yard. This neighborhood was popular for working-class families. The population was primarily White and did not have many Black and Mexican families. There were two major military bases nearby. Many ex-police and military people retired in this area.

During the Great Depression, the community's growth plummeted: businesses closed, jobs were lost, and home values dropped. The streetcar line that transported workers downtown stopped, and the amusement park closed. After sixty years, the state fairgrounds relocated to the northern part of the city, a move that contributed to the area's economic waning.

Homeowners who could not maintain their properties sold their homes and moved to newly built and less-expensive suburbs.

In the 1950s, seventy percent of non-whites lived in the west end of the city, considered the slums. The prior year, Congress passed the American Housing Act in 1949 to increase the standard of living, eliminate slums, and improve housing structures and community safety. The city's white leaders felt they should tear down the west end area and rebuild with federal monies.

In 1954, President Truman's "Fair Deal" housing program gave way to revitalization projects, but there was no attempt to relocate or assist displaced residents who lived in the West End. In addition to urban renewal, the banks exercised discriminatory practices known as "redlining." Mortgage lenders drew a red line around portions of a map to indicate which neighborhoods they will not provide a loan. Redlining became an issue of racial bias in court. Lenders made certain no one could get a loan to fix up their house or buy one in the west end of town. This practice contributed to the overcrowding and physical deterioration of areas with non-white populations.

Covenant is a legal "contract" that affects future buyers of the property. Racially restrictive covenants refer to contractual agreements that prohibit the purchase, lease, or occupation of a piece of property by a particular group of people, in this case, African Americans. These types of agreements are enforced through the cooperation of real estate boards and neighborhood associations. This practice was so prevalent in many large cities that Black families were barred from buying properties.

The West End's minority population dropped by thirty percent when they were forced to move to the Southside. Residents of the West End experienced a racial purge. The properties were appraised at lower values than their actual worth. This widespread prejudice supported the belief that if a neighborhood's population was non-white, then it was worthless. Urban Renewal and Redlining were seen as means to America's racist housing history.

In 1950, this community was ninety-three percent White. During the West End redevelopment, the exiles relocated here. This area did not restrict home and land ownership for nonwhites as other places did. As Whites moved from this town to more modern and spacious homes in the suburbs, a new culture emerged as Blacks opened businesses and renters replaced owners.

In the early 1960s, the freeway expansion, declining property values, and families migrating to the suburbs now became easily accessible. These newly built freeways divided the White community from the Black community. Trees were cut down, and neighborhoods demolished to build the roads. The freeways split the city into smaller sections isolating the Southside area from the rest of the city. A small beautiful town became an urban, crowded jungle. A decline in property values forced people to move outside this area. New, large, low-income families took their place. The old blue-collar jobs that sustained neighborhood residents disappeared. Black businesses opened, and Black religious, social, and organizations increased. Some families could not afford the up- keeping of a home. Over the years, this area took a toll. Buildings became dilapidated, and homelessness and crime were everywhere. Economic problems and social issues intensified.

During the Vietnam War, this area's continual decline brought an increase of crime, such as prostitution, theft, and drug dealing, and with it, a heavier police presence. The city's police department began to enforce a law-and-order-style approach that often led to racial discrimination. This town emerged as an important focus of racial tensions and struggles during the Civil Rights era. Non-white people were treated badly, and it was hard to find decent housing. Very few Blacks lived downtown, and the schools were still segregated.

Tensions between the community and police skyrocketed when officers raided the headquarters of a chapter of the Black Panther Party (BPP), which was known as the Riots. Police brutality became common in this area. Blacks were harassed. The clash between the community and police worsened the relations between the two and led to more businesses closing as people chose to leave the area.

The BPP's purpose is uplifting the Black community. Many people volunteered to help with the social programs. Members were trained in various areas for six weeks. The BPP offered a free breakfast program for 150 school-age children daily, taught Black history classes, tutored children in reading, developed a program for helping prisoners get out of jail, and other volunteer positions in the community.

The police and FBI agents targeted this neighborhood's BPP group. In 1969, when the police were considered as racist, only eleven Blacks were on this area's force of 450 police officers. Their theme was to "Get a Panther." The BPP's office was raided many times with police using tear gas, and the building vandalized. One afternoon started with police patrolling the area and telling people what to do. The police provoked this incident as verbal insults and lewd hand gestures went back and forth between the police and the people. Tension increased. The police armed with shotguns cleared and blocked the street. Many people went and hid in the office. The police lined up in their units and fired into the office. The people hustled out the back door to escape the chaos. Fifteen people were injured.

The following year, a sniper killed a police officer near the office. Four members of the city's BPP were arrested after police alleged that they fatally shot an officer while he was driving through the neighborhood. They were called "Cop Killers." No one had evidence, and a deranged dope addict claimed that he overheard these men plotting to kill a police officer and saw them implement their plan. Doctors and psychiatrists testified that this man is incompetent as a witness as he had brain damage.

The judge allowed him to stand trial and then realized that the medical exam is correct. After an eight-month trial, the four men who served eight months in incarceration were acquitted of all charges. It was all a setup!

During the Vietnam War, twenty-three percent of Blacks and Mexicans served in combat. These men came back from Vietnam by themselves rather than with their units or companies. For a decade, as one person was shipped off to fight, another was returning.

The USA protested against the war in every city, so when these men returned, they were spat upon. Instead of getting "peace" symbol when they returned, they got the middle finger! The soldiers came back wounded, amputated, and mentally incapable of dealing with civilian life.

Along with the protests against the Vietnam War, the Civil Rights Movement intensified. The neighborhood's School of Afro-American Thought was established, the Black Student Union Outreach Center opened, which provided resources and services, and the Black Panther March paraded at the Capitol!

By the end of the Vietnam War, veterans with PTSD almost doubled, and one of five men suffered from mental illness. The community health legislation established block grants to provide services for the mentally ill. The Omnibus Budget Reconciliation Act repealed these grants ending the federal government's role in providing services to the mentally ill.

The Reagan administration closed the mental hospitals and cut mental health funding. The government ended institutionalizing mentally ill prisoners, patients who were forced to enter the criminal justice system. Ten percent of the prisoners have a psychotic disorder.

During the 1970s and 80s, the area became urbanized. The Black and Mexican population increased to eighty-two percent. Homelessness increased due to loss of jobs, unaffordable housing, and steep cuts in welfare programs. Fifty-eight percent of the homeless population had emotional and psychiatric illnesses, of which eight percent were Vietnam Veterans. Many homeless, drug/alcohol addicts, and mentally ill people slowly populated the streets. These people had nowhere to go except to hang out in the local parks, under a bridge, or empty parking lots. Families in this area struggled to meet basic needs, with more than one-third of the families living in poverty. Crime and unemployment rates were high, fueled by gang violence and a poor performing, under-resourced school system. The problems continued in a downward spiral.

ABOUT THE AUTHOR

Connie Steinman is a native of Philadelphia, PA., who has lived in California since 1983. She pursued a film career and worked as a production assistant, location scout, stagehand, and extra in films/TV in the Bay Area. She also produced, directed, filmed, and edited five short 16mm films. Three have been in International Film Festivals, and two are currently on YouTube. Connie is an alumni of FIT (Florida Institute of Technology) Jensen Beach campus and has earned several degrees from other universities including SJSU and CSUS.

She currently teaches American Sign Language and English at the same high school for twenty years and wrote, implemented, and taught the ASL curriculum and scope & sequence for her school district! She has taught all grade levels, including ESL/SDAIE English.

She was one of twelve teachers chosen to participate in UC Davis' Globe Academy to direct students in a scene of *Taming of the Shrew*. The teachers attended a two-week course at the Globe Theater in London to engage in teaching methods to reach students. The final performance included each teacher's class performing a scene of the play at UC Davis Performing Arts Center. She also received the Fulbright Scholarship for the China Institute 2015. Twelve teachers from California were chosen to study "the Silk Road" and its influences from Shanghai to Beijing. They traveled through the Gobi Desert and given a private tour of the Mao Gao Caves, parts that were not open to the public.

She has traveled to India twice for Teach for Peace to learn how to apply Gandhi's philosophy in the classroom.

She has acted in several plays, including *Hair*. Her travels have taken her throughout Southeast Asia, Europe, South America, Canada, and the

Moore, Catherine, Psychologist, MBA. "What is Self-Reliance and How to Develop It?" *PositivePsychology.com*. DOA: 29 March 2020.

Patterson, Nick. Interview. 23 Oct. 2019

Pyke, Alan. "The Lone, Painful History of the Sacramento Neighborhood Where Stephen Clark was Killed." *Think Progress*. Web. 30 March 2018. 23 June 2020.

Russel, Tieon. Interview. 20 Dec 2019

"Sacramento Chapter of the Black Panther Party." PDF File. ND. 30 June 2020.

Sacramento_chapter_of_the_black_panther.pdf

Snow, Kamari. Interview. 20 Dec 2019

Whelan, Richard. *Self-Reliance the Wisdom of Ralph Waldo Emerson as Inspiration for Daily Living*. Three Rivers Press: New York. 1991.

"If one advances confidently in the direction of his dreams,
and endeavors to live the life which he has imagined,
he will meet with a success unexpected in common hours."
—Henry David Thoreau

It will chase after you when you get your own purpose.
Banish the doubt, shut down the dialogue,
cultivate the witness, tame the ego, and trust thyself!
Wayne Dyer